About the author

Peter Coleman began his career as a magazine editor and writer, mainly of books on Australian themes. He was then distracted into politics and Parliament (where he served as a State Minister and Leader of the Opposition). But he saw the error of his ways and has now returned to his earlier vocation. He has also been a director of the Australian Institute of Dramatic Art and the Australian Film School. He has known Barry Humphries for over thirty years.

Also by Peter Coleman

The Liberal Conspiracy
The Heart of James McAuley
Obscenity, Blasphemy, Sedition

The Real Barry Humphries

Peter Coleman

CORONET BOOKS
Hodder and Stoughton

For Verna

The right of Peter Coleman to be identified as the author of this work has been asserted by him in accordance with the Copyright, Designs and Patents Act 1988.

British Library C.I.P.

Coleman, Peter
 The real Barry Humphries.
 I. Title
 791.092

 ISBN 0-340-55907-1

Printed and bound in Great Britain for Hodder and Stoughton Paperbacks, a division of Hodder and Stoughton Ltd., Mill Road, Dunton Green, Sevenoaks, Kent TN13 2YA (Editorial Office: 47 Bedford Square, London WC1B 3DP) by Clays Ltd., St Ives plc.

Contents

Acknowledgements

The author gratefully acknowledges the help of the following people (without attributing responsibility to them for anything written here): Madeleine Armstrong; Liz Bailey; Bruce Beresford; Katherine Brisbane; Stan Brown; Mike Carlton; Tanya Costello; Anton Cermak; Sue Elstub; Margaret Fink; Ross Fitzgerald; Tom Fitzgerald; Les Foxcroft; Cliff Hocking; Rosalind Hollinrake (formerly Humphries); Michael Humphries; Gilda Jennings; Rabbi J.S. Levi; the Hon. R.R.C. Maclellan; Diane Millstead (Humphries); Tony Morphett; John Morris; B. Newton-John; Peter O'Shaughnessy; Warren Osmond; R.C. Packer; Kate Packer; Ray Patterson; John G.B. Perry; Ian Rutherford; Philip Sergeant; the late Ian Sime; Dennis Smith; C.K. Stead; Richard Walsh; Dennis Main Wilson.

The following institutions have also been helpful: the Performing Arts Museum at the Victorian Arts Centre; the Latrobe Library and the State Library of Victoria; Camberwell Grammar School; Melbourne Church of England Grammar School; the Mitchell Library and the State Library of New South Wales; the Denis Wolanski Library at the Sydney Opera House; the Fisher Library at the University of Sydney; the Library of Australian Consolidated Press; the Oral History Department at the National Library of Australia; the Library of the Australian Film, Television and Radio School.

Preface

Sheridan Morley has called for several teams of psychiatrists to investigate the British obsession with Barry Humphries – an Australian actor-writer who often looks like a myopic fairy godmother out of a Fellini nightmare but who packs the halls from the Theatre Royal, Drury Lane to the Palace in Manchester or the Hippodrome in Birmingham or the Royal in Nottingham. When the psychiatrists have completed their research in Britain, it would be another useful public service if they examined the Humphries phenomenon in Australia where his creations erupt and where – despite or because of his love-hate affair with the country – he has for over thirty years staged the most popular one-man shows in its history.

This book does not attempt to pre-empt the psychiatrists' reports, only to offer some raw material or data for their consideration.

I have seen Barry Humphries perform many times since I first, in some surprise at a Melbourne party in the 1950s, watched him shuffle across the floor to clown a singing derelict in a municipal park – and already everyone present knew we were seeing an artist of genius. In the following years I have joined the hundreds of thousands who have enjoyed the performances in small and large halls, in movies, conventions, art shows and book launchings ('Is she the Queen?' a Vietnamese boat person asked me at a recent launching), not to mention the millions who enjoy his television shows (and commercials). I have also seen Barry Humphries put on a bold face at enormous failure, such as at a glittering champagne supper after the movie *Les Patterson Saves the World* died the death of a dog.

One venue sticks in my mind – a poker-machine beer palace and club on the Australian beach resort strip, the Gold Coast. The show followed the familiar pattern, opening with Arabic music and announcements in Japanese and other tongues, the playing of 'Advance Australia Fair' as Sir Les Patterson asked us to give Dame Edna the clap she so richly deserves, and ending with a sign flashing 'Ovate Now!' The audience was not sitting in rows but on chairs at small tables and were smoking or drinking (although no beer was served at tables within reach of Sir Les's spittle) or, when not laughing or ordering drinks, passing asides to each other. After the show Barry Humphries remarked to me: 'This is where it all began', that is, in the music-hall.

He has always resisted the tag of 'satirist' as too pretentious. In all the *Who's Who* entries he calls himself a 'music-hall artist' and many critics have now adopted this description. 'It's as if the music-hall had never been away,' one critic (Michael Ratcliffe) wrote after his most recent London show. But there is also more to it. To be a music-hall artist in the twentieth century is itself an act of protest against the humbug of the age. In other words, like all great comics, Barry Humphries is both an entertainer and a liberator.

His popularity has lasted now for over thirty-five years and reached new heights during his recent sensational successes on British television. He himself is sometimes sceptical about this success. In a comic obituary he wrote under the name of 'Bronwyn Praxitiles', he (she) described the then ancient comic as a self-indulgent and inaudible has-been who lacked any sense of Progressive Social Relevance. That was why in his native land, the critic explained, his work has long been banned by the Australian Democratic Republic's

Art Squad. He endured his last years of exile and obloquy in the tarnished splendour of a Lusitanian spa, occasionally giving clandestine performances to his dwindling, ageing, reactionary and hard-of-hearing followers. He is 'survived by innumerable wives, great-grandchildren and creditors'.

That's as may be. At the moment he is at the height of his powers, the greatest entertainer of the age, with a long way still to go.

1

The Real Barry Humphries?

Reporters who set out to 'interview' or to 'profile' Barry
Humphries usually return to their desks not empty-handed
but frustrated. They will certainly have a 'story' and they
will have been well entertained, but the 'real Barry
Humphries' whom they seek will remain as elusive and
protean as ever. For Humphries, an encounter with a
journalist is always another episode in an unending contest, a
game, for which he has developed a new set of rules – the
Humphries Doctrine of the Interview. The aim of the
interview, he declares, is to shed shadow where once there
was light, to obfuscate what was just becoming clear. Or, as
he once put it more bluntly, he will not take part in the
popular sport of 'perving on the privacy of artists'.

Sometimes he may appear candid and co-operative. 'What
is there to say about me?' he will ask in bewilderment. 'I
don't smoke. I don't drink. There must be some way you can
jazz me up.' At other times he will be ingenuous: 'I am
Church of England. I wash my car on Sundays!' Or
obscurantist: when asked if comedians tell the truth, he
replied: 'No. They distort it to tell a more accurate lie.' Or
oracular: 'Being oneself is a form of disguise.' He may
assume any of a variety of masks: a monocled Edwardian
dandy, a moustached Ronald Colman in yachting gear, a
surrealist hidalgo, a gothic student of Prague. The Holly-
wood biographer Charles Higham, who found Humphries a

driven character out of Edgar Allan Poe, was confused by his sudden changes of mood, from relaxed mildness to lethal hatred. One representative journalist, after reporting one of Humphries' disarming performances, concluded that just when you think you may be getting close to the artist, you realize that you are only getting close to the role he is then playing (which may be the role of Barry Humphries in a confidential mood). Another said his trick is to make journalists feel they are in on the joke but in fact they are the joke.

His press conferences are even greater spoofs. At one – a mid-morning champagne brunch to launch a record album *The Sound of Edna* – Humphries appeared at the podium before the legions of reporters wearing the mask of a seedy, monocled impresario, in a rumpled morning suit and chewing a bent cigar that spilt its ash freely. You must approach Dame Edna in the correct way, he lectured the reporters. Stand back when she enters the room. Curtsy. Do not be pushy. Do not speak until spoken to. Do not try to take her gloved hand unless it is offered first. The squalid impresario then withdrew and almost immediately a frizzy-haired Dame Edna arrived on a Honda motorcycle in punk gear, a tattered black T-shirt beneath a black leather jacket, a razor blade dangling from a chain around her neck. She proceeded to sing: 'S and M Lady':

> Shave half your head, paint your legs green.
> No one's too old for the S and M scene.
> Drive them insane, frighten the vicar,
> Swing that chain with the big swastika.
> S and M ladies, let 'em all go to Hades.

At another conference, to launch *An Evening's Intercourse with Barry Humphries* in Sydney, he played host for forty-five minutes to 160 champagne-sipping reporters in his hotel suite. When he withdrew, Dame Edna was discovered in a hot spa and agreed to take questions. One reporter asked: 'What do you think of the new legislation to reform the rape laws?' After a long, fixed stare, Dame Edna pursed her lips, and replied: 'Where do I come in?' to roars of tense laughter. Another reporter turned away, to avoid the grisly sight of his peeking, slavering colleagues. (In any case the one-man show grossed millions of dollars.)

At yet another — for the launching of the show *At Least You Can Say You've Seen It* in Melbourne — he hired a tram and invited the press on a picnic to celebrate the bursting of the wattle, the Australian harbinger of spring. Each had to wear something as yellow as wattle (or bring an oriental friend) and as the tram weaved through Camberwell Junction yellow drinks were served — pernod, advocaat and sherry. At lunch in the Wattle Park chalet, the journalists were served creamed sweetcorn, curried egg and daffodil-yellow jellied trifle, after which Humphries recited his Betjemanesque 'Wattle Park Blues'.

> Back in the wattled thirties
> Before the world went dark
> They built this noble Chalet
> On the crest of Wattle Park . . .
> And so dear friends and strangers
> I presume to be your guide,
> To the terminus of memory
> I have shouted you a ride,
> To the place where I, and Colin,
> And a thousand kiddies more
> Picnicked underneath the pollen
> In the days before the war.
> Today the trees seem shorter
> And the cable trams have gone,
> But they still serve, in the Chalet,
> Melbourne's finest buttered scone.

The reporter who tries to break through the fantasy or folderol does not get far. One presenting himself late at what Humphries calls his third act – the one back in the dressing room after the two acts on stage – demanded bluffly: 'When did you first start playing this role?'

'What can you mean?' said Dame Edna, mascara now running down her face. 'When I was born.'

'Well, when did you start to dress up like this?'

'They've sent the wrong man,' Dame Edna sighed loudly, turning away – and the journalist gave up.

On another occasion an Australian reporter interviewing Sir Les Patterson began by quoting with approval his taxi-driver's criticism that Humphries presented only a few characters, unlike another well-known comedian – a television mimic of public figures – with a great repertoire of impersonations. Sir Les replied slowly ...gradually settling his pay-back: '...Yes, we live in a land where the taxi-driver as drama-critic is an interesting phenomenon ...You are probably right ...Brian [sic] Humphries really hasn't the talent for impersonations ...he has to make his characters up, plucks 'em out of his brain ...performs 'em in London ...maybe with a team of writers he might be better. I don't know ...why not go outside, grab a cab and ask that bloke?'

In fact, only one among Humphries' countless interviewers in several countries seems to have been able to lift the mask that Humphries was wearing at that moment, and that was Andy Warhol in very special circumstances: the flop, due largely to the *New York Times*, of *Housewife-Superstar!* in New York at Theatre Four, not long after its colossal success in London where half a million people saw the show. Dropping his guard for the moment Humphries said: 'I just couldn't go through a failure at forty-three. I mean why should a person as talented as I have to perform in a deconsecrated church in the heart of Hell's Kitchen and be reviewed by the former foreign correspondent to Madrid?

Why should I go through this?' Then collecting himself
again, Humphries offered some advice to the young:

> One must never resent the unfavourable review one might
> receive; and no matter how disappointed or wounded the
> artist really feels, he should never display any feelings of
> animosity or verbalize them to members of the press. This
> is very bad for the image and may be considered crude or
> tasteless. I've always had the odd stinking review —
> everywhere. I'm no exception. But I've never let an
> unfavourable notice affect me. I read them and forget
> them. Put them out of my mind for ever. Remember, it's
> just bad luck if the person who doesn't get you happens to
> be an influential journalist with five children and a
> clubfoot.

But this interview remains exceptional, an Andy Warhol
rarity.

There is little point in the journalists consulting Barry
Humphries' many autobiographical statements. His entries
in various editions of *Who's Who*, for example, are, like his
programme notes or Dame Edna's recipes, minor literary
genres of their own. They provide some information and
hint at more. In various entries he describes his schooling:
'Self-educated, attended Melbourne Grammar School'; his
ambition: 'arousing the lions of laughter'; and his profession
(or quest): 'profiting from strange concealments'. It is here
too that he describes his principal — and renowned —
reaction: 'Inventing Australia' an Australia which is as real as
James Joyce's Dublin and as much a synecdoche of
civilization. But the entries soon become as much a game as
his interviews and obfuscate as much as they clarify: in one
entry his publications include *Les Putaines Sataniques. A
consideration of minor Baudelairean book illustrators in
Belgium*, a study which has eluded collectors and bibliog-
raphers, whether Baudelairean or not. In another he

nominates as sole relaxation 'listening to early twentieth-century Swedish Chamber Music' – a predilection of which his musical friends had been entirely unaware. In still others he has acknowledged only two marriages when there have been three – now four with the marriage at Spoleto in June 1990 to the writer Lizzie Spender, daughter of the famous poet Sir Stephen Spender.

A more useful approach to the Humphries phenomenon appeared in Gambier, Ohio, in 1964 in a prophetic parable based on the life of Barry Humphries, who was then almost entirely unknown outside Australia. Called 'A Fitting Tribute', and written by a New Zealander, C.K. Stead, who had known Humphries in Auckland, it appeared in *Kenyon Review*, a journal published by a liberal arts college of Episcopalian disposition. Since one of the parable's themes is the inevitable gulf between the Artist and the uncomprehending State, Community and Press, it quickly enjoyed a certain fame in translation in dictatorships such as Spain and Hungary. But the theme is and is meant to be universal.

The artist in the story, Julian Harp, is easily recognized. In one Humphriesian episode, Julian, a disreputable-looking young man in a tattered, buttoned-up raincoat, takes the narrator to an Auckland disco where the patrons jeer at his clown's appearance and call him Jesus. 'Julian laughed too and clapped in a spastic kind of way and looked all round like a maniac as if he couldn't see who they were jeering at.' Then he stood up and began to jerk and twist and stomp so superbly that the crowd stopped jeering, made a circle around him and began to clap wildly until, exhausted, he could dance no more.

Julian invented a set of characters who regularly wrote letters to the newspapers as part of his 'Subvert the Press' Campaign. His plan was to take over the letters-to-the-editor columns and then bring down the government by using the letter-writers in a co-ordinated attack. He wrote the letters in a sort of daze, as if hearing voices. But gradually the characters took on their own lives. They would no longer agree with each other. Some supported, some opposed the government. Some even began writing letters to his girl-friend, saying he should be hanged or flogged, although one wrote that it was only his mind that was disordered.

The climax of the story is Julian's inspired success in doing what no man had ever done before: flying like a bird using wings of his own invention that were initially propelled by the springs of stolen umbrella struts. When, after months of gruelling training (and public discouragement), he finally took off at a gymkhana sponsored by two charities, the Blind Society and the Crippled Children's Society, he soared across the vast Pacific disappearing over the horizon in the Hauroki Gulf. Even when he tried to come down, he could not: whether it was because of a fault in the wings or because Julian was in a trance or because there was somewhere he wanted to go, 'there was no way to go but higher and further until his energy was used up'.

The final irony is that now that Julian is world-famous and believed to be dead, the State, supported by the press, has taken over his reputation, commissioning statues, odes, paintings and presenting him in a suit and tie as a clean-cut, short-haired National Hero. Those who knew him recognized the falsity of the official legends. They knew him to be an unkempt drifter, a graceful aesthete, some sort of thief and the father of an illegitimate child. But they also knew him to be a man obsessed who worked in 'a daze' and 'a trance'. Yet if they said so, they were treated as liars or madmen and silenced. The public did not want these facts, but it craved a legend, just as the artist did not face the world directly but used invented characters, coded messages and masks. Even the narrator, his companion, collaborator and the mother of his child in the end accepted this: 'Soon I learned to say nothing about Julian. He belongs to the public and the public makes what it likes of him'. Even she did not 'know' him (although she knew more than most) and she could not explain his soaring flight. Her last remarks apply as much to her as to her readers: perhaps if your umbrella was stolen, 'it may mean you contributed a strut to the wings that carried him aloft'.

Unlike Julian Harp, his model, Barry Humphries, is not only alive but enormously popular. He also shows few signs of becoming a National Hero (although he has been honoured by the Queen and his government as well as by his profession). But like Julian Harp, 'he belongs to the public and the public makes what it likes of him', however wrong that may be. His characters also have their own reality like Julian Harp's letter-writers in his 'Subvert the Press' Campaign, and his artistic flights remain as mysterious as Julian's. We can track his career from Melbourne to Megastardom but we know this will only illuminate a strut of 'the wings that carried him aloft'.

Some thirty years ago the present writer attempted to translate Barry Humphries into the language of journalism or daily life. As an assistant on a somewhat pretentious magazine (printed, as Humphries might have said, on butcher's paper), I asked him to elaborate, in an article, his scorn for the insipid philistinism of a newly created, government-funded theatrical entrepreneur. When he delivered his article in his mannered, recondite, decadent prose, I knew it would never be accepted by my comparatively pedestrian publication which insisted on clear, direct, informative and usually short sentences. I rewrote the article in the style of the magazine. Humphries shrugged his acceptance (and sent me a copy of Richard Garnett's *Twilight of the Gods* with an introduction by T.E. Lawrence). In due course the article appeared. I am still pleased to have helped put on record Humphries' criticism of the Australian stage in that critical, formative period of his career, but I also know that the published article lacks all the intensity, *élan*, colour and bite of his original. The style is the man. Barry Humphries is his masks.

2

A Gothic Childhood

John Barry Humphries, a Saturday's child, was born to John Albert Eric Humphries and Louisa Agnes (née Brown) on 17 February 1934, a date which figures from time to time in his sketches, usually a grim or absurd occasion such as a drunken father's collapse at his daughter's wedding or a trendy cleric's Divine Revelation.

In a *Baby's Record* of *art nouveau* design, a doting mother noted her first-born's weekly weight and height and recorded when he first sat, crawled, stood, fell, spoke, teethed or put his toe in his mouth. Lists of aunties and uncles were also recorded as they assembled for his special occasions: the christening (at St John's, Camberwell Junction) or the first birthday party. (He later claimed that Mrs Everage is a composite of all the aunties who ever poked their heads into his pram.) There are many photographs of a smiling, if occasionally exasperated, infant.

He grew up, with a sister and two brothers, in the comfortable Melbourne garden suburb of Camberwell — 'hideous heartbreaking Camberwell', as he once described it in a nostalgic ode which ended:

> Oh Camberwell Town Hall look down
> On this your City, once a town,
> And then before that, vacant blocks
> Where no one thought of planting phlox

Or building Ampol petrol bowsers
Or stucco'd Spanish Mission houses.

Yet ever in my mind you'll dwell —
Hideous, heartbreaking Camberwell,
And ere I take Extremest Unction
My soul will flash back to 'The Junction'.

— although he almost always refers to pre-War Melbourne
with nostalgic affection: 'enchanted by distance, intact,
before the rot set in. There it is, ante-bellum Melbourne . . .'

The family home was 36 Christowell Street (his principal
characters, Edna and Sandy, always settle down at number
36, after some early uncertainties), recently built high on the
hill of an old golf course. It was a posh street, made of
cement not bitumen, and the Humphries house was
two-storeyed, neo-Georgian cream brick. The garden including the grass was English: one of Humphries' earliest
childhood memories is of gazing out of his bassinet at
honeysuckle and 'I knew one day I'd be going to England'. (It
was an England of pre-Raphaelite landscapes that lured him,
not the England reflected in boys' adventure magazines such
as *Champion* or *Triumph*, which left him cold.) The family
was prosperous, conservative, Church of England, the
Federal Member of Parliament was Robert Gordon Menzies,
later Prime Minister, and later Sir Robert, Warden of the
Cinque Ports. ('It's moments like these you need Menzies'
was a slogan the student Humphries later offered to the
Liberal Party in a parody of the advertising of a famous
Australian sweet: 'It's moments like these you need Minties';
the offer was not accepted.)

But if the suburbs of Melbourne helped shape and colour
Barry Humphries' vision, there was little in the history of the
Humphries family to prepare it for this visionary. The closest
to either stage performers or scourges of the age were some
Methodist ministers among his Lancashire forebears. (One

great-uncle wrote *The Old Testament and its Message*.) His father, a native of Benalla in Victoria's Ned Kelly country, was a builder who took his child to inspections of building sites and gave him the feel for house-and-garden fashions and fads that he turned to such advantage later. Both sides of his family were large (if England is the mother-land, he later wrote, and Germany the father-land, Australia must be the aunty-land) and the child experienced many huge family parties with their great quantities of cakes and scones prepared from the family recipes. (It was at gatherings of this kind that he gave his first theatrical performances, wearing, he recalled, a tea-cosy or a saucepan.)

The family was soon aware of the prodigy it had nurtured. How could it avoid the tensions associated with his emerging artistic cast, will and aloofness? Humphries inevitably disliked and quarrelled with almost every educational institution that he attended, from kindergarten to university (not to mention his three months' National Service in 1953 in the Army, which nevertheless noted Private Humphries' 'amazing imagination and originality' and made him scenic designer for the Puckapunyal camp concert.)

Kindergarten was noteworthy for presenting him with one of his enduring theatrical and literary themes: deformity and guilt. One lunch time, on his bike, he bumped into another boy who fell, breaking an arm which, being crudely reset, remained withered for life, and a constant reminder to Humphries of his role in the malformation of the unfortunate child. At his first school, South Camberwell State, his sense of isolation deepened. He detested the school and still does. In particular there was the Miss Jensen Incident. Miss Jensen, perhaps simply noting the boy's self-will, found occasion to punish the six-year-old by standing him in a corner with a sign around his neck: 'I am a bully'. Humphries believed that he was entirely innocent of any offence (and even twenty-five years later, Miss Jensen's name turned up in a programme note: he was still planning, he pretended, an elaborate, incomprehensible, bewildering vengeance). But at the time he did not mention his grievance at home and was puzzled, even then, at 'this mysterious lack of rapport' which had opened up between his parents and himself.

His artistic gifts flourished, however, at his next school, a small private school, which he unreservedly enjoyed: Camberwell Grammar, where he seems quickly to have won the contest with the school authorities who came to call him, alone in the school, by his Christian name. (He disliked the triumphalist, galumphing sound of his surname.) It was at this school that he learnt the pleasures of eccentricity, stimulated by a post-Impressionist art teacher who talked about Van Gogh and drove a Tin Lizzie. He took up easel painting (on masonite provided by his father) and his blackboard caricatures of his teachers were acclaimed. Here too the teachers encouraged his literary gifts. His first published poetry at the age of seven, a verse on Mother's Day ('May all the day be happy, pray/and all the sweet birds sing') appeared in the school magazine (which rejected one of his poems on the ground that it was so good that it would only discourage the others). His first published prose also appears in this magazine: gothic sketches of rumbling thunder, blinding sun and stinging dust. His was altogether a gothic childhood: if his school satchel carried cheese sandwiches and half-pints of milk, the newspapers carried front-page war pictures of piles of bodies, of people hanging from lamp-posts, of devastated cities. One Scripture teacher, Stan Brown, was so impressed by the promise of the boy's dramatization of the Last Supper ('Where's that rat Judas Iscariot . . .? I've never liked the look of him!!') that, contrary to school rules, he put the exercise aside, preserving it for posterity as a literary curiosity.

Those relaxed Camberwell days inevitably came to an end, and in 1947, at the age of almost twelve, he became a day-boy at the famous Melbourne Grammar. There he entered a tougher world of compulsory football and cold showers, of discipline and Empire. Melbourne Church of England Grammar (or simply Grammar) is an Establishment school with ivy-covered walls which has produced several Prime Ministers, Premiers and other public figures. During the war its official song proclaimed, 'Praise ye those who stood for Britain'; its staff organized the boys to prepare food and soap parcels for Britain; and its magazine published lists of 'Our Honoured Dead'. After the war an editorial in the magazine declared: 'Let us be a little louder in proclaiming that we are British subjects, living in the British Empire, under the British flag.' The Anglican Archbishop, Dean and Archdeacon of Melbourne are all members of the school council and the school's blue cap bears a white bishop's mitre. The writer and diplomat Graham McInnes for one complained that supercilious Grammar boys conducted themselves in the streets of Melbourne as if they owned the place, as indeed their fathers largely did.

Most of Humphries' published memoirs of Grammar are as of a nightmare – of hearty bullying prefects and unsympathetic or mediocre teachers. He recalls, for example, a Neanderthal school captain (in later years, as he liked to imagine, a travelling salesman for a cheap brand of port) caning him in a bookless 'study' for dodging football: 'The game's up, Humphries!'

The Headmaster or 'Boss' was also an awesome figure of enormous, but not limitless, authority; when in an excess of disciplinary zeal, one expelled some boys for misbehaviour, the parents obliged him to resign.

Yet these adolescent years at Grammar were also enlivened by Humphries' artistic turbulence, especially in painting, poetry and acting. His landscape oils won school prizes and were reproduced in the school magazine ('our star oil painter'). A leader in the school's Art Club, he invited famous artists such as the communist, Noel Counihan, and the pacifist, Max Meldrum, to speak to the club, and in 1950 he himself delivered an extraordinary address on the history of the modern movement in music, millinery and above all painting from *les fauves* to post-War abstract art. Is this all for the better? the sixteen-year-old asked. 'We must wait and watch.' In 1951 he arranged an exhibition of students' original Dada works, including his own first versions of 'Eye and Spoon Race' and 'Mona Lizard'. The exhibition provoked, he reported, 'much sincere and earnest comment'. He also produced at this time a series of Dadaist black-and-white cartoons and sketches, some of which have survived. In one of them a gross, ebullient master of ceremonies in a radio quiz show is welcoming a limbless war veteran: 'How about a big hand for one of our boys from Korea!' Another shows the artist asleep at a desk on which stands a glass and empty wine bottle.

In poetry he published many (prize-winning) poems in the school magazine and, even if, as he later complained, several were bowdlerized, they were all the work of a true poet perfecting his craft. Their spirit is a *fin de siècle* gloom, their technique modernist, under the influence of T.S. Eliot, Siegfried Sassoon and the Sitwells. They have titles like 'Failure', 'Futility', 'Lament from the Tomb'. These examples will suffice. In 'Heritage' (1950) he writes:

> We all inherit burdens brain-inborn:
> Great unaccomplished tasks to us appointed:
> Tormented too are we by that same scorn
> Which forged the failure of the first anointed.

In 'Life's Illusions' (1950):

> A million Mr Noahs
> Sail on doveless seas:
> A legion of church-goers
> Drain the loveless lees.

In 'Failure' (1950):

> The air is filled with eyes of men who failed:
> Opened in madness, death, in suicide they stare
> As each cold meteor flies into space.
> Grieved eyes grimace
> As where a comet cleft,
> The slow inevitable skies close without thunder.
> I press my frantic eyes into the deep,
>   comfortless pillows of eternity.

and in 'Revised Version' (1951; inspired by a newspaper report from Hiroshima describing the scientific interrogation of survivors):

> Ere God destroyed the cities of the plain,
> Abram went out and searched the streets in vain
>   For ten just men —
> So all within were slain.
>
> We in our wisdom wait and let the dust subside;
> Till sun has sucked safe the bomb-poisoned air.
> Then with transfusions (and a questionnaire),
> Set out to save the few who haven't died.

But it was his performance in the school plays, his first public performances in real roles, that attracted the most attention, especially his female impersonations. The school favoured English farces, by Ian Hay, Walter Hackett, Arnold Ridley. His début was a brief part in 1948 as Mrs Brash, a miner's wife, in Ian Hay's *A Safety Match*. Carrying her baby, he/she looked amazingly like the early Mrs Everage. The (anonymous) school critic commented on 'a fiery glare in his [her] eye', and reported that 'J.B. Humphries held the stage with a strong and vigorous sketch'. A year later he had a fuller role as Mrs Pengard in Walter Hackett's *Ambrose Applejohn's Adventure*. The critic reported that 'he played superbly and with magnificent aplomb so that for moments at a time his true sex was forgotten'. The following year his third female role was Julie Price in Arnold Ridley's *The Ghost Train* and again the critic reported that his portrayal of this 'obsessed, strange woman of the world who breaks into the play so dramatically' was 'excellent'. His final role at the school was a male one: the instructor or 'schooley' in *The Midshipmaid* by Ian Hay and Stephen King-Hall. This too was 'an assured performance', equalling, the critic said, his 'unsurpassed' interpretations of 'female parts'. In the picture accompanying the critique, Humphries, in horn-rimmed spectacles, wearing a coat of mail and carrying a helmet, easily stole the show.

Humphries finished his Grammar years with a good liberal schooling as well as a self-taught catholic grounding in the gothic writers and the *poètes maudits* including the English ones from William Beckford to Ronald Firbank – a tradition to which he felt himself drawn. The result of his final public examination was spectacular and one of his examiners – the critic and novelist R.F. Brissenden – has told of his pleasure and relief at coming across, in the long stretch of semi-literate mediocrity, one of Humphries' English papers: written in a large flowing hand in purple ink, the answers had little relation to the questions but were 'dazzlingly sharp and intelligent and revealed a bizarre knowledge of some of the more obscure areas of English literature', including Beckford's *Vathek*. After discussing the problem the examiners agreed to give him top marks.

The school magazine proudly published a picture of him – although for years afterwards he dismissed the school as a branch of the Junior Chamber of Commerce, its aspirations expressed in the motto *Crines Longi Crines Foetidi* – Long Hair is Dirty Hair. Before Humphries went on to Melbourne University, the Headmaster sent for him and asked, eyelids drooping, 'Barry, I hope you're not turning pansy?'

3

The Distant Roar of Edna Everage

Few people needed or wanted a university degree less than
Barry Humphries. In his two years, 1952–3, at the University
of Melbourne in the student generation that included
Germaine Greer, he 'studied' or read law and then arts, but
he completed no courses and passed no examinations. Yet he
created a legend that lingers still.

It was at this time that, pursuing his interest in Dadaism
which had emerged at school, he discovered Robert Mother-
well's book of 1952, *The Dada Painters and Poets, An
Anthology*, and he adopted its aesthetic nihilism as the
organizing – or disorganizing – principle of art and life, of his
hoaxes, revues, exhibitions and politics. One contemporary
recalls his Ubuesque impersonation of Adolf Hitler in a
student revue: tall, gaunt, sallow, hypnotic-eyed, with
forelock on forehead, passionately declaiming the word
'Dada' over and over again until the audience could take it
no longer. Another recalls a sketch in which Humphries
played a politician who is about to speak from a stump but
constantly drops his notes. 'Ladies and gentlemen', he would
begin, 'I am not here . . .' and he would drop his notes again.
. . .Even his performance of the Welsh peasant, Evan Howell,
in a student Drama Festival production in August 1953 of
Emlyn Williams' *The Wind of Heaven* became a solemn Dada
spectacle as he passionately proclaimed the Lord's Prayer in

Welsh (and in full, more than the text required) in Adelaide's Tivoli Theatre, his first stage triumph and one that planted at least the faintest hope of a theatrical career.

In 1952 he published his own Dada Manifesto, inspired by Tristan Tzara, proclaiming:

> Cubism was a school of painting, fascism a political movement, DADA is a state of mind.
>
> Free-thinking has no resemblance to a church. DADA is artistic free-thinking.
>
> We are incapable of treating seriously any subject whatsoever, let alone DADAism.
>
> The Acts of Life have no beginning or end. Everything happens in a completely idiotic way. That is why everything is alike.
>
> Simplicity is called DADA. So, like everything in life, DADA is useless.
>
> DADA is working with all its might to introduce the idiot and the cretin everywhere. And it, itself, is tending to become more and more idiotic.
>
> DADA is terrible; it stinks, it feels no pity for the defeats of the intellect or for the high cost of living.
>
> DADA proclaims that there is no relation between thought and expression!!
>
> The word DADA means as much as you do. DADA is always using the bathroom. It sometimes goes to sleep in church. DADA uses its Bible for a telephone book – it loves little kiddies. DADA moves at 33 revolutions a minute – it enjoys long-playing bilious attacks. DADA takes Vincent Van Gogh's with CONFIDENCE!!
>
> DID YOU DADA YOURSELF THIS MORNING?
>
> P.S. – Do you disagree with all this? Then you are one of us!

In accordance with this creed he staged two art shows in 1952 and 1953 with such exhibits as 'Beethoven's Last

Movement', 'University Lecherer', 'Pus in Boots' (a military boot filled with custard) and 'Now We Are Sick' (a bucket filled with what appeared to be vomit). The musical background was provided by placing a gramophone at each end of the gallery and arresting current hits with a piece of string attached to a pick-up arm so that Mary Martin kept singing 'And you will note, I've a lump . . .' or 'I'm in love . . . I'm in love' (with a wonderful guy). Another gramophone played a laughing record. The *Time* art critic Robert Hughes later said of the shows that their 'ferocity and point might have pleased Tristan Tzara'. (At least one work drew blood at the time, to Humphries' delight: 'Old Fool's Tie' – a Melbourne Grammar tie around an empty Abbott's lager bottle. When an indignant Old Boy of Melbourne Grammar seized it, Humphries announced the loss on a loudspeaker, 'explaining' that the thief was unhappily under the impression that the bottle was full.)

He inevitably stood for the Students' Representative Council elections as a 'Men's General' candidate on a Dada platform: 'Generally speaking, I am a man and vice versa. I wholeheartedly support National Service [and] condemn International House and the Aboriginal Scholarships. I support (or oppose) a Korea Peace. I consider the whole of the University should be rebuilt on the lines of the present Wilson Hall [a new, ugly building]. Being a schizophrenic I feel qualified to represent all shades of University opinion. Dada for now.' When he was defeated, he declared the result 'a great triumph for Dada'.

One critic, Graeme Hughes, in an early memoir caught something of the legend Humphries was cultivating: 'Rumours began to circulate . . . He was reputed to live in a darkened incense-filled room, and to drink crème de menthe out of his shoe. He had been seen wearing six-toed gloves on his feet in public transport. He was the reputed possessor of rare recordings by Schoenberg and an original Charles

Conder. It was even said that he was engaged upon the composition of an opera based on Franz Kafka's *The Metamorphosis* and that he had purchased at great expense the complete works of the Marquis de Sade, bound in human skin ...' Most of these rumours, the writer avowed, were 'wonderfully true'. (It was at least true that as a schoolboy, he had bought two original Conder lithographs, both signed and numbered by the artist.)

Humphries' series of hoaxes, or unpractical jokes, deepened the emerging legend. They were early expressions of street theatre and, judging from Humphries' repeated emphasis on them, they meant a good deal to him. Some were funny, although more in the acting than the telling, others less so; some actually happened, some are apocryphal; all were thought of – at least by Humphries – as changing the victims' lives by breaking the mould of their convention-al expectations. Some began as simple games: if some drunks sneered at his then unfashionably long hair, he might sometimes stammer an abject apology for his incurable scalp complaint which made hair-cutting impossible, or at other times rise to apparently crippled feet and limp miserably to the door – in either case leaving the sneerers silent and ashamed.

Others were more complex. In one, recorded as 'The Ashburton Line Affair', he took a seat in a non-smoking first-class compartment on an early morning Melbourne suburban train. At each stop a uniformed waiter would pass in a course of breakfast: first grapefruit, then cornflakes, followed by bacon and eggs and finally coffee. Not a word was said. According to uncertain legend, the effect on the other passengers was shattering.

On another occasion, also in a train, a colleague with a white stick, dark glasses and a leg in plaster, entered a crowded compartment and was immediately offered a seat where he proceeded to read a pianola roll. Humphries, in black coat with a black hat over his long hair, also stepped into the compartment and began to read a foreign-language newspaper. As the train lurched he fell over the plastered leg. In a rage he then began beating the leg with his stick, shouting: 'You blind, crippled Australian bastard!' Once more, according to uncertain legend, the other passengers were never quite the same again.

The most Dada or anti-bourgeois of all his hoaxes was proffered as an attempt to undermine the basis of commerce – the role of money as a medium of exchange. According to the legend, a Mr Malouf ran a small goods shop near Melbourne University. Each day Humphries would go in, buy a cake of Lux soap and, after handing over the money, would leave the soap on the counter. Mr Malouf would call out: 'You've left your soap', and Humphries would reply: 'I don't want the soap. I only wanted to buy it.' Mr Malouf, as we are told, nearly went crazy. After several weeks of this, Humphries finally took away the soap, but then returned saying: 'Mr Malouf, I forgot to leave the soap,' and left it on the counter. But he had substituted a cake of lard for the soap. He never returned to the shop, but imagined that someone would buy the lard in Lux wrapping, plunge it under his armpit, find it was lard and complain to Mr Malouf who might then think he had some sort of clue to the mystery, although he hadn't. Humphries considered it a sophisticated exercise in mystification. 'I don't know of any parallel to it', he later said. On the basis of it he quickly invented a Malouf Memorial Library and a Malouf concerto, and over thirty years later a Professor Malouf wrote the introduction to Les Patterson's *The Traveller's Tool*. If by the 1980s it seemed to Humphries a 'not very sensitive thing to do when one considers the feelings of the shopkeeper', it remains one indicator of his frustration and rage in the 1950s.

However, the most prophetic of all the Dada happenings at Melbourne University at this period was the first intimation of Edna Everage. In September 1952 Barry Humphries staged a Dadaist revue titled *Call Me Madman!* (after Irving Berlin's *Call Me Madam!*) in the University's Union theatre. Humphries has recalled the event in numerous, if unreliable, articles, essays and interviews. On his account, the revue's overture — one musical phrase played over and over again on an untuned violin — was followed by the principal sketch, 'The Indian Famine', in which Humphries played the berserk wife of a missionary, both of whom were seated at a table laden with raw meat, vegetables and cakes. The missionary read aloud the awful statistics of a current Indian famine and the wife responded in an increasing falsetto: 'I don't care ... I've got plenty of food ... lots of food ... and they've got nothing ... wogs, nigs, yids ...' As the husband intoned more and more terrible figures, the wife's cruel, hysterical and uncontrolled laughter grew even louder, until finally the quarrelling pair began to throw chops dripping with blood and cakes dripping with cream at each other and at the members of the audience who, in turn, flung the food back to the stage or around the auditorium, while a voice continued to broadcast the famine statistics over the amplifiers.

In Humphries' memory, the grim satirical point of it all eluded the affluent students who, in the great tradition of Dadaist happenings, now stormed the stage after his blood, while a portable gramophone ground out 'God Save the Queen' at various speeds and a woman in a nun's habit stood on stage swearing, with infantile gestures, at the audience. Humphries remembers escaping the students' wrath by hiding in a broom cupboard (or, in another version, fleeing in a waiting taxi). The metropolitan Press, he recalls, condemned this episode of student tastelessness and the Union authorities banned the Humphries' group from further use of the Union Theatre.

Other eyewitnesses have entirely different memories. They

recall an ill-written, ill-rehearsed lunch-time turkey which a small audience soon abandoned in boredom or irritation. They recall no wild indignation, no storming of the stage, no condemnation by the metropolitan Press and no bans by the Union authorities. Yet, whatever the facts, Humphries' memory, or fantasy, is the better guide to the future, for much of his later showmanship is in this early attempt at anti-theatre: the surrealistic zaniness, the assault on the audience, the growing hysteria, the fantastic climax – and the black image of man's pain and cruelty. Edna Everage is not present, she has indeed not yet materialized, but her spirit hovers heavily over the spectacle – a genteel beast, its hour come round at last, slouching towards Moonee Ponds to be born.

4

Made in Melbourne

Edna Everage was indeed born not long afterwards, but at first she was little more than an idea without a name, address, clothes, husband, children or mother. Far from being the thrusting pest of the 1960s, let alone the international *monstre sacré* of the 1990s, she began life as a strident ridiculous housewife, a pantomime dame, a Mrs Malaprop from Moonee Ponds. She was a party turn, an in-joke among Barry's friends.

But party turns buttered no parsnips in what was for the pale, fey, long-haired twenty-year-old artist, the oppressively philistine city of Melbourne. 'Vocation, like a hair-cut, loomed menacingly,' he recalls. 'At any moment now the cruel barber would whip the sheet off some scalped and sheepishly grinning youth and yell, "Next please" to me.'

He composed his farewell to his youth in a Sitwellian parody which concluded:

So it's goodbye Othello, old fellow
We never may see you again.
May you dance all your rumbas
In the Café Columbus
For ever and ever, amen.

– and in 1954, 'one of the most dismal years of my life', took a job, 8.30 a.m. to 5 p.m., with the international record

company, EMI. It was the year of transition from 78 records
to microgrooves and the company had decided, for reasons
to do with copyright, to destroy the old stocks. Humphries'
orders were to smash them with a hammer, everything from
Wagner to the Ink Spots. He saw it as a Dadaist act and went
at it, hammering away, with an insane frenzy, spurred on by
an executive who told him to hammer harder. It produced,
he recalled, 'a more acute form of nervous exhaustion than I
had experienced in my less compulsory Dadaist activities'.

To relieve the tension he turned at night to the newly
formed Union Repertory Theatre company at Melbourne
University, for which he played small roles in two English
plays. One was Lord Robert Tyrwhitt, a reptilian court-
intriguer in Jeanette Dowling's and Francis Letton's *The
Young Elizabeth* (a play chosen to help the new company
take advantage of public delirium over the Queen's first tour
of Australia), and the other, Colonel Dobrieda, a bemedal-
led colonial chief of police in Dorothy and Campbell
Christie's *His Excellency*. His performances brought mild
praise, although Humphries still had no serious thoughts of a
stage career. But more importantly it was at the Union Rep
in 1954 that the Melbourne-born Shakespearian and actor-
producer, Peter O'Shaughnessy, 'entered my life'.

Ten years older than Humphries, with experience of the
English repertory theatre in the early 1950s (a wilderness
against which he warned aspiring actors) and a man of wide
culture who shared Humphries' love of music and painting,
he recognized his promise, encouraged, instructed and
criticized him, and finally urged him to consider a stage
career. For some five years Humphries was almost
O'Shaughnessy's apprentice. One programme note stated
simply: 'He [Humphries] first studied acting with Peter
O'Shaughnessy.'

When Humphries made his first brief and rarely acknowledged marriage in October 1955, it was to another actor in
an O'Shaughnessy production of *Love's Labour's Lost*,

Brenda Wright. The marriage was celebrated in Melbourne's graceful Wesley Church decorated by two biblical paintings by Rupert Bunny; the bride – a dancer as well as actress – wore a bouffant ballerina dress of white chiffon and a short Giselle-style tulle veil; Mrs Shirley O'Shaughnessy was her attendant and Peter O'Shaughnessy a sort of unofficial best man.

As Humphries' talents and confidence grew, the pupil-master relationship with O'Shaughnessy could not survive, and almost inevitably it ended in some bad blood and some lawyers' letters. But it was in this period that Humphries found his métier as an actor-writer and as the creator of Edna Everage, Sandy Stone and the rest of the Humphriesian family.

O'Shaughnessy cast Humphries as a languid, toadying undergraduate Rosencrantz in his production of *Hamlet* late in 1954; then as the stammering suitor in *Le Malade Imaginaire*; and finally as the humourless pedant Holofernes in *Love's Labour's Lost*. He believes that it was while Humphries was playing these roles that he learnt 'technique', especially control of his voice (which, O'Shaughnessy complained, had a tendency to sputter and quaver) and picking up a cue. It was at this time too that John Sumner of the Union Rep invited him to play the lovesick Orsino to Zoë Caldwell's Viola in a country tour of *Twelfth Night* in Victoria. This was Humphries' first engagement as a full-time professional actor (at six pounds a week) and it released him from EMI. But it was not good casting: he seemed, said one critic, like a man suffering from indigestion 'who should be saying "If Dexsal be the cure for me ..."' Another observer described him as 'a tall, stooped, long-haired and beady-eyed figure whose skinny legs completed an overwhelming impression of an Elizabethan emu'. The director said later: 'Imprisoning Barry in a script was a terrible job. But his performance was always interesting, even if not quite what we expected.' At least it was an Orsino that made people laugh.

It was while travelling from country town to country town in the Rep bus that Edna finally emerged with her own name and inane gentility, if not yet a surname. Since the tour was sponsored by the Victorian State Council of Adult Education, the company was officially welcomed and offered entertainment in the various towns, usually by the Lady Mayoress, and as the bus moved on to the next town Humphries would do his turn, parodying the recent 'entertainment' and previewing what was in store for them. But Edna remained a company joke.

Back in Melbourne he played a number of other roles for the Union Rep, including the swaggering cowboy Kit Carson, with an enormous moustache and a ten-gallon hat, in William Saroyan's *The Time of Your Life* and the wise, ironic and cheerful old waiter in George Bernard Shaw's *You Never Can Tell*. But it was on 13 December 1955 in the Christmas revue, *Return Fare*, that on the suggestion of the director Ray Lawler (whose own play *Summer of the Seventeenth Doll* had been the Union Rep sensation of 1955) Humphries first presented his Edna Everage of Moonee Ponds on stage. It was a two-handed sketch called 'Olympic Hostess', written by Humphries for a Melbourne preparing to be host city to the 1956 Olympics. Mrs Everage, slimming in preparation for the Lovely Mother Quest and wearing a charcoal suit with a large chartreuse cabbage rose in her revers, informed an urbane Games Officer, Mr Hopechest, that she was willing to do her bit by billeting various visiting athletes 'from England and overseas'.

MR HOPECHEST: 'How many rooms comprise your home, Mrs Everage?'
MRS EVERAGE: [taken aback, laughing] Oh, gosh – I'll have to count them! Let me see now [counting on fingers] there's our bedroom, of course – Norm, that's Valmai's

father, has just painted it a lovely shade of duck-egg blue, and the bird's-eye blonde three-piece looks lovely against it, and I've just bought a new chenille bedspread in a sort of pinky colouring —

HOPECHEST: Very attractive, very attractive I'm sure, Mrs Everage, but you surely don't wish to share your bedroom with the athletes?

MRS EVERAGE: Oh, goodness, no. Norm isn't as sporting as all that, but you see, it's just off the main hall, and they're sure to peep in every now and then —

HOPECHEST: [doubtfully] Ah, I see. But to return to the number of your rooms, Mrs Everage —

MRS EVERAGE: Ah, yes. Well, there's our bedroom — one. Do I count the hall?

HOPECHEST: No!

MRS EVERAGE: There's our bedroom, one — then there's the lounge and dining room. If you open the double doors — little Kenny — that's my youngest — always calls them the reindeer doors because of the sand-blasted reindeers on the glass — if you open the double doors it's a lovely big room. We pushed back the Genoa velvet couch and rolled back the burgundy Axminster for Valmai's twenty-first, and the young people had the time of their lives —

In due course the Games Officer raised the question of her preference among nationalities.

MRS EVERAGE: [confidentially] Look, little Kenny would really be tickled to death if you could let us have a real Red Indian.

HOPECHEST: [firmly] I'm very sorry, Mrs Everage, but the only Red Indian in the Olympic contingent has already been accommodated at Pascoe Vale.

MRS EVERAGE: Oh! The poor little kiddie will be disappointed. Never mind, I know it's not your fault. Well now, I'll read you our other choices. Valmai: Rhodesian,

Dutchman, British. Norm: Canada, American or — Eerie.
Merv — that's my son-in-law — said he was easy, but that
he wasn't too keen on the idea of Mau Maus. Bruce
suggested —

Finally, after contemplating the various terrible possibilities,
her native xenophobia prevailed and she settled on Whites
Only ('Remember the Policy!'), preferably Aussies. She
swept out, leaving Mr Hopechest an exhausted wreck.

Edna's family — her mother, Norm, Kenny, Bruce, Valmai
— all appear in this first 1955 sketch, although their later
miserable fates in Edna's triumphal backwash are not yet
evident. The sketch was successful, but only moderately; it
was one of several good sketches in the Christmas revue, and
neither Humphries nor his audience had any intimation that
Edna had an astonishing future, or any future at all. But it
was success enough to point Humphries in a new professional direction. The Union Rep director John Sumner
advised him to give up dramatic acting in Melbourne and to
try intimate revue in the new Phillip Street Theatre in
Sydney. Or as Humphries put it some years later, in a piece
of anniversary doggerel:

When told how old this Company was, I scarely could
    believe it.
For it seems only yesterday that I was asked to leave it.
I couldn't learn my lines, you see, which wouldn't do at
    all.
So I was driven to a sordid life in the sleazy music-hall.

Since those far days the wound has healed; I've learned
    to weigh all factors
Although I but a comic be, I don't envy real actors.
Of bitter dregs I've drunk enough; of fame I've sipped
    the cup.

They still have lines to learn by heart; I have to make
them up.

Humphries also recalls the heavily accented advice of a
fellow actor, from Prague: 'Barry, an actor needs to have it
here [he tapped his head] ... and here [the heart] ... and
here [the lap].' After a pause he went on: 'You have it here
[the head] ... but ...', and then he shrugged. William Orr,
the producer and driving force of the Phillip Street Theatre,
offered Humphries and his wife roles in a new show, *Mr and
Mrs*, and they moved six hundred miles north-east to
Sydney, to a new planet.

5

Around the Loop in Sydney

Edna Everage once dramatized the cultural gulf between Melbourne and Sydney in this memoir of 1976:

> On a recent trip to the Old Country I met a rather sophisticated-looking Australian woman. She sat beside me on the plane smoking like a chimney and reading (I could not help noticing) one of those paperbacks with an unnecessary picture of nudists on the front cover.
>
> I might add that my unfortunate travelling companion was seldom without a drop of something in her glass, and although she was smartly dressed in an obvious way, her pantihose were snagged and her nail polish was badly chipped. It was then that a tiny voice inside me whispered some words I instinctively knew to be the truth: 'Don't look now, Edna,' it said, 'but the tipsy frump beside you hails from Sydney.' Sure enough, after we had exchanged no more than a few words I learned that the drink-crazed ragamuffin on my right was no refined Melbourne lass: she came from Sydney all right, and though she was absolutely typical, she was a terrible advertisement for that interesting dockside town. On learning that I hailed from the Victorian capital the sozzled strumpet set out to be deliberately rude.
>
> 'The only time I ever think of Melbourne,' she declared through a haze of filthy ciggie-smoke, 'is when I have to

think up an excuse for not going there.'

I bit my tongue. I merely smiled politely and inquired if Sydney's recent plague of cockroaches had found their way into that white elephant of an opera house or bitten many nude bathers on Sydney's notorious pervert-haunted beaches. How glad I was that my mother taught me to turn the other cheek and counter insults with pleasantries.

Each city has tended to define itself by contrast with the other. If Melbourne is refined, self-controlled, temperate, anglophile and wet, Sydney is raffish, boozy, free-thinking, chauvinist and sunny. Typically, if Melbourne established a professional repertory theatre in its University in 1953, Sydney opened Australia's first full-time theatre of 'intimate revue' in the heart of the city, in 1954.

The Phillip Street Theatre, a 300-seater doing eight shows a week, was brash, irreverent and topical, with new lines daily to mirror the headlines. It attracted most of Australia's best comic talent in acting, writing and composing, including Max Oldaker ('the last of the matinée idols'), Gordon Chater, Reg (then Reginald) Livermore, June Salter and Wendy Blacklock. It gave Barry Humphries his first opportunity to develop his cabaret style.

He played in two revues for Phillip Street, in 1956 and 1957, and his first Christmas play for children, *Alice in Wonderland*, in which he was the Mad Hatter. The first revue was *Mr and Mrs* (the gimmick being that the stars were four married couples) in which Humphries and his wife Brenda shared several acts. Mrs Everage also made her Sydney début in a revised 'Olympic Hostess' and, as in Melbourne, audiences found Edna quite, but not particularly, amusing. Although the review did not run for long, it remains noteworthy that one critic, Josephine O'Neill, singled Humphries out as 'the comedy discovery' of the season.

The next revue, *Around the Loop*, ran to full houses for twelve months – far too long for Humphries. Edna Everage made another short appearance with the comic verse 'Colour Question' about the then trendy colour, maroon and its universal and inexplicable mispronunciation in Australia. (It contained the first reference to the banishment of Edna's mother to a 'Twilight Home'):

> All our family loves it and
> You ought to see our home.
> From the bedroom to the laundry –
> Every room's *maroan*!
>
> When we bought our home in Moonee Ponds
> It didn't have a phone
> But it had one thing to offer:
> The toilet was maroan.
>
> The day my mother had her turn
> We heard an awful groan
> I dropped young Ken, dashed to her room
> And there she was – maroan.
>
> And now she's in the Twilight Home
> We're going to England soon.
> But one English custom gets my goat
> They call maroan 'maroon'.

He also presented a new monologue in which Edna warned the authorities, with a growing threat in her voice, that the proposed spectacular Sydney Opera House must provide play-centres for kiddies and for the screening of fine films like *Carmen Jones* or else . . .

I quite enjoy a bit of opera myself. Now and then. As a matter of fact I remember not so long ago taking my little kiddie along to see *Carmen Jones* when the picture was out our way and it was a really nice night's entertainment for the little lass. A real education, too.

But the sketch did not catch on and was dropped after a few performances.

It was soon clear that, however valuable the training he received at Phillip Street, the company did not have the bite Humphries was looking for. There was too much name-dropping, too much ingratiating to socialites and (in those pre-television days) to radio 'personalities', and too many sketches taken from London revues with only perfunctory changes of names and places. It was 'intimate revue' of a self-congratulating kind, and Humphries' ideas were frequently turned down. It was not surprising that one of his scenarios, in which a restaurant diner finally submits to the insistence of his lady and the management that he remove his top hat, only to reveal a hideous cancerous growth, was rejected. The exposure of concealed horrors was not in the Phillip Street's style. But another sketch in which Humphries lampooned the Sydney press for its disgusting harassment of the artist-composer-conductor Eugene Goossens, who had pleaded guilty to importing obscene articles, was also timidly rejected.

If Humphries sometimes complained of Phillip Street's bland middle-class values, he was really asking for more than it was able to give. It was a frustrating period for him. His first brief marriage was breaking up. He did not respond to Sydney's younger Bohemians, apart from particular individuals such as his close friend the artist Margaret Elliott (later a well-known film-producer, Margaret Fink): he was to describe most of them as 'a forlorn and excruciatingly feeble group of punters and toss-pots' whose artistic and literary legacy was nil and who seemed united only in their 'interest in shoplifting, abortions, SP betting, wife-swapping and disdain for Culture'. As for the older Bohemia, it was at this period that the great Sydney poet, Kenneth Slessor, looked up from his billiards and asked, 'Why don't you get your bloody hair cut?' (It took him, Humphries wrote later, thirty years to see the joke. Others are still trying to see it.) He had Christmas dinner (as he recalled) at the home of a famous English actress, whose Sydney-born gigolo thereupon importuned him for a cash contribution towards costs. Sydney, Humphries wrote, reflecting on those years, 'for all its larrikin vigour has always provided the artistic fraud, copycat and plagiarist with the most generous, even affectionate amnesty of any provincial centre'. In Australia, he decided, it may be a state of grace to be distrusted, even hated, and he wrote to O'Shaughnessy obscurely about the need for 'some heroic act of espionage'.

He planned indeed several acts of espionage. One was his assault on Australian complacency through his creation and refinement of the Typical Australian; not the rugged, bronzed digger of legend, rather a humdrum but lyrical, disappointed but reconciled, limited but decent little old man from the suburbs. Called Sandy Stone, he was to grow into a universal figure, one of the most touching expressions of suburban life since Charles Pooter in George and Weedon Grossmith's *Diary of a Nobody*.

Like Edna Everage he emerged slowly, piece by piece, and did not make his way to the stage easily. One early aspect of him is dimly seen in 1956 when Barry Humphries was booked to perform at a Sunday morning smoko in a working-class poker-machine casino and beer hall called the Granville Returned Servicemen's League (RSL) Club. He travelled to this outer suburb by train with an experienced and encouraging older actor who briefed him about the sort of audience to expect. But on arrival at the Club, Humphries was chilled to hear the roar of the batteries of poker-machines and to observe several rows of hung-over men with faces out of Cruikshank or Rowlandson, downing their heart-starters. To the 22-year-old aesthete, the Melbourne Grammar boy and the revue artiste it was a bizarre new world. Since he had no regular act to perform, he had decided to try out one of his Expressionist party turns – a harrowing piece in which an androgynous, ghostly cretin called Tid (a character developed in collaboration with his fellow Dadaist, John Perry) is being interviewed by a kindly psychiatrist, both parts played by Humphries. In the act the roles are gradually reversed until finally the doctor collapses and the child walks away confident and cheerful. Barry Humphries' companion from the train warmed the crowd up with his mouth-organ and a few shaggy-dog stories, and when Humphries stepped on to the stage there was an expectant hush. In one version (published in Scotland) the act went like this:

'Tid,' the Doctor cautioned, 'I'm afraid we'll have to give you some special therapy exercises for fear you'll grow up different from other boys.'
'Whee,' said Tid gaily.
'Now, Tid, I want you to count up to ten.'
'Whee,' repeated Tid.
'Don't be scared, we'll do it together. Are you ready?'
DOCTOR: One
TID: Whee!
DOCTOR: Two
TID: Thiths
DOCTOR: Three
TID: Eeee
DOCTOR: Foour
TID: Fooffh
DOCTOR: Fife
TID: Fiff
DOCTOR: Schix
TID: Schicks
DOCTOR: Pr--r-r-r-r

TID: Scheffen
DOCTOR: Djee-djee
TID: Eight-t
DOCTOR: Jub
TID: Ninne
DOCTOR: Swissf
TID: Ten!

'Gee, thanks, doc. I feel as if you've made a new man of me,' lied Tid.

'E-e-e,' replied the Doctor truthfully.

'Well, I'll have to be getting along now.' 'E-E-E,' wailed the Doctor.

After Tid had gone home, as wrong as ever, the Doctor said 'Bub-bub' and died.

Shortly after he began, most of his audience rose, one by one, to return to the pokies or the bar, and even those who remained to listen lost the rest of his act in the noise and uproar. It was a resounding flop, and on the strained train journey back into town, Humphries' companion tried to console him: 'You don't *have* to be a comedian, you know. There are plenty of jobs around for a young bloke like you.' But the Granville failure turned out to be one of the most productive experiences of Barry Humphries' life. He had observed many elderly Tids in his Granville audience — lost, bewildered, wandering, droning old boys — and the idea of merging them with the diggers of the RSL, of fleshing out his Tid with suburban detail, began to take tentative shape.

Humphries soon stumbled on the character's voice: one winter afternoon at this time, near Bondi Beach where he was then living, he asked the time of a wiry, elderly fellow 'with thin sandy hair and rosy, finely capillaried cheeks, two-toned cardigan and a pair of freckled marsupial paws'. The sturdy, matter-of-fact 65-year-old replied in a cracked, drawling falsetto voice which was just the intonation Humphries needed for his character-in-the-making. At the same time he decided to call him Sandy (Alexander Horace) Stone, with beachy overtures and an echo of a popular radio detective, Randy Stone.

A little later he elaborated Sandy's way of life, his world, in a short story which was finally published in an obscure students' magazine in Canberra in 1958. Called 'Sandy's Big Week', the story was the character's first public appearance. It was signed H. Grahame. In it Sandy is a ghostly figure in a bulky white shirt and khaki shorts, who is watering the flowers in the evening shadows while, inside, a lamp lighting his wedding photograph has turned it into 'a vacant pane of glass'. He has been married to Beryl for twenty-eight years, and their world is one of cards, tennis, the RSL Club, wireless, church, sponge fingers . . . He relaxes in his burgundy crushed velvet armchair, blowing smoke at a kookaburra painted on the lampshade. 'You've got to be in it to *win it!*' bellows an unreal voice from the wireless. Sandy said he would . . . buy some cashews at the Junction.

The character did not really begin to take off until he was given voice, however frail, in the 1958 record, 'Wild Life in Suburbia', with the monologue 'Days of the Week'. Beginning in his plaintive drawl: 'I went to the RSL the other night and had a very nice night's entertainment,' Sandy proceeds to outline his week: at the club, at the pictures, the slides night, the cards night, the Lodge, the footie. The week ends as it began with 'a nice night's entertainment', and Humphries' pleasure in bizarre turns of language lightened the narrative: 'I don't say no to the occasional odd glass'; 'Beryl makes a lovely sponge finger'; 'You wouldn't catch me missing an important semi'. But sometimes such a phrase takes on a darker meaning and becomes a reminder of the human condition, of our lot: describing his afternoon at the football, at the semi (-final), he slowly mutters: 'It's very cold and blowy in the outer' – and, suddenly, in the subsequent silence, we are all in the outer, cold and blown . . .

The record was widely acclaimed in Australia and Humphries followed it up with two new recorded sketches. In one, 'Dear Beryl', Sandy is writing to his wife, who is visiting the Old Country, and he passes on the news:

> Mrs McLeod 'fell asleep last Tuesday'; 'the big hyder-angea's (*sic*) a goner'; and old Jim Longmire still has his 'tummy trouble': his son's 'mixed marriage' (to a Roman Catholic) had nearly killed old Jim who has 'spent a small fortune on that boy's education. Grammar and one thing and another.'

In the other, 'Sandy Agonistes' there is no narrative or action at all, only the quavering recital of ante-bellum advertising slogans, headlines, public figures, snatches of song and especially brand names: Cure 'em Kwik, Dr Morse's Indian Root Pills, Carter's Little Liver Pills, Kiwi Boot Polish ... It evoked in tears and laughter a lost age, the simpler if narrower time before, as Humphries put it, the rot set in.

Sandy Stone, in these recordings, was the first of the Humphries' characters to catch the attention of English critics, even before they had seen him on stage. Julian Jebb wrote that the effect of Sandy's litanies is 'anthropological' – as if the listener is 'present at the construction and decay of a mythical society'. Colin MacInnes wrote that the message of the soliloquies is: 'The dream-in-reality, the marvel-in-drabness which is our lot, which only an artist of rare originality can reveal.' John Betjeman described Sandy as 'a figure whose prototype can be found in most parts of the Western world, the decent, honest, kind-hearted but deeply conventional man who takes life as it comes' – a verbal and Australian Charlie Chaplin.

It took many years before this view was more widely shared outside Australia and Sandy Stone still does not have the magnetism of Edna Everage or Les Patterson, let alone the television megastardom. He is one for the lonely tear

Above left: Off to school, *circa* 1943, with sister Barbara. This picture was taken on the neo-Georgian front porch of the family home in Camberwell, Melbourne. (Note the dependable Globite school case.)

Above right: With younger brother Michael and paternal grandfather J. G. Humphries, *circa* 1947. (Note the Windsor knot in the Melbourne Grammar tie.)

Below: The Conservationist, *circa* 1945 at Balwyn Sanctuary.

Standing, second from left, as Mrs Pengard in a school production of Walter Hackett's *Ambrose Applejohn's Adventure*, 1949. One critic said he played this precursor of Mrs Everage with such aplomb that 'for moments at a time his true sex was forgotten'.

Front row, fifth from right, as bespectacled 'schooley' in the 1951 school production of *The Midshipmaid* by Ian Hay and Stephen King-Hall.

Above left: With his first wife, Brenda Wright, in 1956. A publicity shot for his professional début in the satiric revue, *Mr and Mrs*, at Phillip Street Theatre, Sydney. (*John Herder*)

Above right: As Estragon, left, with Peter O'Shaughnessy as Vladimir in Samuel Beckett's *Waiting for Godot* at the Arrow Theatre, Melbourne and the Independent Theatre, Sydney, 1958. This was the first professional production of Beckett in Australia. (*Phillip Stainton*)

Below: Sydney Bohemia *circa* 1956, with Margaret Elliott (later Fink), at Pakie's nightclub, about 2 a.m.

At an ossuary
in the environs
of Prague,
1972.

At home in
Little Venice,
London, *circa*
1967, with
some of his
Charles
Conder
collection in
the
background.
(*Lewis Morley*)

With Salvador Dali in Gotham Book Mart, New York, 1963. (*Phillipe Halsman*)

The earliest surviving photograph of Mrs Everage, 1958 (although she had been created three years earlier, in 1955).

Mrs Everage during her first appearance in 1962, wearing her characteristic eyewear. (*John Tourrier*)

With his second wife, Rosalind Tong, at a 1965 press conference before the opening of his show *Excuse I!*

The Dadaist. 'Dr' Humphries at his 'retrospective' art exhibition in the Victorian Artists' Society Gallery, Melbourne, 1958.

rather than for outrage or disgust. Yet as Humphries takes him through the theatres of the cities and towns of England and Australia, he is convinced, from the audiences' responses, that he is reaching Everyman. Sandy Stone remains very close to Humphries' heart and it is impossible to take his measure without this favourite character.

But while he was still sketching his outline and only beginning to flesh out the skeleton, in 1956 and 1957, Humphries remained at Phillip Street in *Around the Loop* which looked as if it would last for ever . . .

6

Waiting for Godot

When *Around the Loop* finally closed in August 1957, Barry Humphries returned to Melbourne, as if liberated, for a series of productions with Peter O'Shaughnessy which, far more even than his Phillip Street experience, transformed his career. The shows began with Samuel Beckett's *Waiting for Godot*, included a popular success – the Australian children's play, *The Bunyip and the Satellite* – and ended with a topical revue *Rock 'n' Reel* in August (and November) 1958 which launched the international career of Edna Everage. It was an *annus mirabilis*.

For Humphries, Samuel Beckett was already a literary master and *Waiting for Godot* – in which two diseased, gabbling tramps, a sort of Dada Laurel and Hardy, exchange neo-vaudevillean and poetic absurdities in a wasteland where they are doomed, stoically, to go on waiting – was a 'magical' work of art, humanist and optimistic: the tramps wait but do not give up. He had discussed the play with O'Shaughnessy for months, as they followed reports of its production throughout the world, especially in London and New York. In London, despite the gibes of Sir John Gielgud ('a load of old rubbish') and the refusal of Sir Ralph Richardson and Sir Alec Guinness to accept roles in it, Kenneth Tynan and Harold Hobson had proclaimed its greatness far and wide, and in New York, despite the vendetta of Walter Winchell and others, it ran to packed houses for ten triumphant weeks, and panel discussions involving the actors and prominent literary figures were held at night on stage after each performance.

They did not expect such a response in provincial Australia. They hoped at most to make a dent in the mindless blandness of Australian theatre. Even the fiasco of the recent production in Miami, Florida, when angry patrons formed queues to demand their money back, would have been preferable to indifference. In any case the play obsessed them. For the Melbourne production they walked the streets dressed as tramps with sandwich boards to advertise the play and in Sydney they stuck 'Godot' stickers on posts, windows and brass plates, especially near the Phillip Street Theatre. 'There's never been a play like it,' Humphries said. Looking back, O'Shaughnessy thought that it changed both their lives.

Humphries played the anguished simpleton Estragon (the role in which in New York, Bert Lahr had given, according to Kenneth Tynan 'one of the noblest performances I have ever seen') and O'Shaughnessy the more hopeful Vladimir. Humphries also designed the sets, being determined to avoid the 'Oliver Messelish' set which Beckett had disliked in Peter Hall's London production of 1955. In Melbourne he scoured the scrap-yards and back lanes for rusty tins, old prams, bicycle wheels and other relics to hang from the flies, and later, in Sydney, in a frenzy of action painting, he hurled mud and rags at a disused and shredded pastoral scene on a back wall which when lit and draped with a fishing net became a 'magical' wilderness.

In the event the play was received with the overwhelming indifference they feared — or half-expected. It ran for two weeks in Melbourne, to about fifty patrons a night. Occasionally an audience was enthusiastic, although often the only satisfaction the actors received was when an indignant patron stormed out: one such woman warned the ticket-seller that one of the actors clearly had venereal disease. The mainstream Melbourne critics ignored the production. The Sydney critics were more effusive but the houses were even smaller, about fifteen a night — an attendance not helped by the actors' practice, at least by now partly contemptuous, of baiting the audience by prolonging the silences unendurably, each sigh or groan from the stalls representing a sort of triumph ...

(The present writer was among the sceptics at the time. As an apprentice-reviewer I brashly wrote in a Sydney fortnightly magazine: '*Waiting for Godot* is about the Human Predicament and all that jazz ...Everything about this production is good except the play. Beckett makes his point very well in the first act and the second act adds nothing whatsoever except tedium. The philistines are right again: the play, or rather, the second act, is a hoax.' I would not entirely recant, even now, and I have since learned to treasure some elaborate hoaxes. O'Shaughnessy replied by asking when the philistines were *ever* right and declaring that Beckett was trying to reveal the psychological state of Western Europe. Humphries' reply came some years later, in 1962 — with the ridiculous nose-picking, toe-picking beatnik guitarist who sang:

> I really get sick of, like nobody has
> The human predicament and all that jazz.)

However, their next major production, the Australian children's Christmas play, *The Bunyip and the Satellite*, in which Humphries played a clown in search of his identity, was a smash hit. The play has never been revived, certainly never in its original form, because of disputes over authorship and rights, but in 1957 it was hailed as contributing to an Australian theatrical revival along with such other successes of the 1950s as Ray Lawler's *Summer of the Seventeenth Doll*. It was Humphries' outcast Bunyip which created the sensation. As he played it, this legendary

Aboriginal swamp creature became one of the great theatrical fools in the tradition of Harlequin, Pierrot and Lear's Fool.
In the Melbourne *Age* Bruce Grant described him as 'a
delicate hero, a courteous, gay, troubled creature', whose
only ambition is to find his identity (animal, vegetable or
mineral) and whose sad, white face with its gum-leaf tiara
and motley, feathered arms and legs painted by Arthur Boyd
inspired feelings 'too deep for laughter'. The Bunyip *was*
Humphries; at the least he was as O'Shaughnessy put it,
'very close to Humphries' secret heart', and something of
the confused and gentle Bunyip survives in most of
Humphries' characters, even, very occasionally, in Dame
Edna. (The production also starred Rosalind Tong, a New
Zealand dancer whom Humphries married as soon as his
divorce from Brenda was settled.)

Humphries and O'Shaughnessy still had confidence in the
public future of Edna Everage and they tried her out again in
April 1958 at an arts festival in the Victorian country town,
Wangaratta. But although their two-man show was well
reviewed and Humphries played vignettes of Iago, Justice
Silence and O'Casey's Joxer Daley as well as an increasingly
ad-libbing Edna Everage, it was O'Shaughnessy's readings
from Charles Dickens and from the Australian writers Henry
Lawson and C.J. Dennis which impressed the critics. When
the local newspaper declared 'Wang Sees a Great Actor', it
meant O'Shaughnessy who clearly 'overshadowed' Humphries and Mrs Everage.

Back in Melbourne (after taking *Godot* and the *Bunyip* to
Sydney) they began the topical revue which was to make or
break Edna Everage. Indeed the first, short version of the
revue, held in a 'churchy' Presbyterian city hall, almost
broke her. It was a lunch-hour show in which O'Shaughnessy and Humphries were again joined by Humphries' future
wife, Rosalind Tong. It was a flop. Edna Everage as the
Olympic (or Migrant) Hostess and as the critic of the Opera

House, made only a slight impression on critics and public, although the more she abandoned her scripts and ad-libbed her way through, the more the small audiences responded. Sandy Stone did not appear at all. At the last moment – influenced by advice from all sides that Sandy was not funny enough and by his own doubts that Humphries' delivery was turning the character from a naturalistic, suburban butt into an abstract-expressionist exercise in futility (too much Tid) – O'Shaughnessy got cold feet and dropped the idea. The audience, O'Shaughnessy said, never made a quorum: 'It's just not funny,' actors, critics and patrons assured him.

Yet within weeks, the situation was transformed and their next show, *Rock 'n' Reel Revue* at the New Theatre in August was a sensational success. Now almost entirely ignoring the script, Edna the ad-libbing monologuist took off with a vengeance. The show began with the Opera House sketch and ended with her urging the adoption of 'Home Sweet Home' as the national anthem. In between Sandy Stone finally appeared on stage (against continuing advice), seated, in pyjamas and dressing gown, in a dimly lit Genoa velvet armchair to overcome the problem of Humphries' height. Nostalgic snatches of 1930s songs ('When I Grow Too Old to Dream', 'Always') punctuated his account of the days of his week and when he droned his last lugubrious words 'a nice night's entertainment', the audience hit the roof, as did most of the critics. Humphries is 'worth our special attention' pompously announced the *Age*, and the evening *Herald* reported: '. . . it will be surprising if Melbourne can resist going along to see itself'. The historian Manning Clark was only one who felt 'that marvellous experience of being in at the creation of something that was to leave a mark on our society'. The influential editor and man-of-letters Stephen Murray Smith said Humphries was the first great new comic to develop in Australia 'since the hey-day of the legendary Mo' (Roy Rene). The architect Robin Boyd wrote: 'He is one of the funniest men you could find this side of hysteria' and the composer Dorian Le Gallienne declared: 'If we had any sense we would pay him a huge retainer to spend the rest of his working days telling us where we have gone wrong.'

Barry Humphries had now broken through. Where was he to turn next? He made two 'Wild Life in Suburbia' records of Edna and Sandy monologues and he put his Bunyip on children's television. He starred in two television revues (in one of which he lampooned a University pundit who had just returned from leading a women's delegation to Mao's China). He did two more shows with O'Shaughnessy, one in Albury in January 1959 and one in Melbourne in February 1959, and he made a television commercial for a breakfast food. But he was really marking time. He had no future with the Union Rep or the Phillip Street Theatre, let alone in the microwaved West End productions beloved of 'the Firm' (J.C. Williamson's) or other Australian entrepreneurs. He had no confidence in the newly established Australian Elizabethan Theatre Trust whose *Lola Montez* he ridiculed for its namby-pamby glossiness. He quarrelled with the Australian Broadcasting Commission and he needed relief from the somewhat autocratic direction of Peter O'Shaughnessy. Australian theatre was in a particularly shoddy period – a life-savers' march-past or a horse-race was better theatre, according to the poet Hal Porter – and Humphries saw few signs of change.

Meanwhile in London the theatrical world was at the height of what Harold Hobson called 'The Great Uprising', led by Bertolt Brecht, Samuel Beckett, John Osborne and Harold Pinter among writers and by the English Stage Company at the Royal Court Theatre in Sloane Square, Bernard Miles' Mermaid Theatre at Puddle Dock and Joan Littlewood's Theatre Workshop at Stratford East, among companies. London was once again a world theatrical centre and mere self-respect alone would have compelled Barry Humphries to emigration.

Early in 1959 he married Rosalind Tong (in an artist's studio), took his shots for smallpox and cholera, collected his British passport, Commonwealth of Australia (born Melbourne; age 25; married; height 6 feet; eyes brown; 'visible peculiarities' none) and with Rosalind caught the steamer *Toscana* for Venice, and then on, via Athens, to London — and obscurity.

7

From the Madhouse to the Funeral Parlour

Barry and Rosalind Humphries arrived in London in June 1959. It was the finest summer of the century but they only had fourpence between them, and a letter from Max Oldaker of the Phillip Street Theatre introducing them to Charles Osborne, the young Australian editor, critic, poet and above all actor with wide experience in England: 'He's a very strange man in many ways,' Oldaker wrote, 'and I'm not sure I understand half his material, but, you know, I think he's got genius. Do give him any help you can. His name is Barry Humphries.'

The Humphries moved, with the Australian artist Francis Lymburner, into a basement flat in Notting Hill Gate and took what temporary, unskilled jobs they could find – he briefly (with another Australian artist, Lawrence Daws) on a night shift in an ice-cream factory, removing, he reported, defective raspberry ripple from a conveyor belt of ice-cream, she – the steadier breadwinner in this early period in London – in a fruit shop. By day Humphries called on his (and his wife's) agent Myrette Morven and 'delightedly' explored London's 'highways and byways' including both the revolutionary new theatre ('the Great Uprising') and the last performances of London's traditional music-hall, especially at the Met in Edgware Road. (Randolf Sutton was 'the most impressive thing I saw'.) He also discovered English pubs and his drinking increased. ('In Australia I had always looked on pubs with some dread as licensed urinals. They smelled of piss and Australian lager.') Since it was also Swinging England he swung enough to join the show-business contingent in an Aldermaston march.

But the first year in England passed without theatrical work except for the short Christmas season as Jonas Fogg, the madhouse keeper in *The Demon Barber* at the Lyric, Hammersmith. The critics noted his vigorous performance in an evil top hat, if only barely. Alexander Bland enjoyed the 'riotous trio in the Peckham madhouse' (that is, Jonas Fogg and his two Vile Myrmidons), and Caryl Brahms, who didn't like the melodrama, liked Humphries: 'Mr Humphrey [*sic*] was out of his teeny madhouse mind something 'orrible.' The show only ran for three weeks and although the producers intended to move it to the West End, the plans fell through.

The same fate awaited another musical, written by Caryl Brahms and Ned Sherrin (who were just beginning their long collaboration) about the fate of Dr Crippen, in which Humphries and Maggie Fitzgibbon were offered roles. Humphries sang (or, as Ned Sherrin put it later, croaked, wheezed or gravelled) some music-hall songs. But Wolf Mankowicz pipped their plans for a place in the West End with a similar tale, his ill-fated *Belle*. (Sherrin recalls Humphries at this period as a 'quiet, courteous and kindly' man ...but 'behind-the-hands rumours of mental distress and alcoholic excess swirled around him like a morning mist.')

In June 1960, however, Humphries finally made his West End début at the New Theatre in a long engagement as Mr Sowerberry, the undertaker in *Oliver!*, a musical version of Charles Dickens' *Oliver Twist* by Lionel Bart, 'the Offenbach of our time'. (Humphries was also the understudy to Ron Moody's Fagin.) It was steady work; Bernard Levin admired his 'witty and grisly' performance, especially the gallows-humour of his rendering of the song 'That's Your Funeral' amid the coffins; and 'many of that glittering West End throng found it impossible to recall Barry Humphries' performance early in the first act,' as he himself put it, 'without pleasure'.

But it was also a dead end, as he looked like being stuck in the role for years. Twelve months is the longest anyone should spend in any show, he said at the time, thinking as much of *Around the Loop* as of *Oliver!*, but 'I cannot escape the devastation area of this "smash hit" because of my contract signed on an empty stomach.' It is all right for earning a living, 'but a show conceived for the box-office, which runs for a very long time, involves the actors in a dispiriting thing rather close to hack work. Managements should realize this and be more sympathetic when their artists seek release from their contracts (after a reasonable period) in order to do another show.'

To hold his interest in the role month after month he experimented with his acting, tried out new ways of saying lines, polished and thought up fresh 'business'. 'My colleagues in this long run,' he told one interviewer, 'tell me to relax and let my "technique" carry me through, as though it were an automatic mechanism devoid of personality. My method is to hurl myself physically on to the stage and to attempt to hurl my very larynx into the auditorium.' (He added, ironically, that some of his colleagues who tried his method lost their voices permanently – 'but I feel that their attempts to live by my high standards have benefited them morally and artistically.')

Years later, in 1989, he told a student audience that, although he 'hated every minute' of playing Mr Sowerberry, he had learned a lot 'unconsciously' from the practical experience of boredom that is 'inevitable in our industry'. 'You should never consider yourself too good for any role from television commercial to soap opera', he then counselled. At the time, however, he declared (in a parody of high-minded 'socially conscious' criticism): 'I disagree with the morals of *Oliver!*, and musical comedy, however "light" is a persuasive influence in the community. That the little hero Oliver should triumph because of his aristocratic blood, and eventually distribute wax fruit to his more roughly-spoken playmates of workhouse days is a vile contention.'

Meanwhile he continued adding to his menagerie of Australian characters, particularly drawing on the rich, crowded and at that time unrecorded world of Australian expatriates in London, the Kangaroo Valley generations who, brought up on a mindless self-congratulatory nationalism at home, were bound to end in comic conflict with the smug and patronizing English in their 1950s mood of profound complacency. One of the first to go public – on the record 'Sandy Agonistes', not on stage – was Buster Thompson, an affluent lout pub-crawling his way through Europe and his Western heritage before returning to Melbourne to settle down in the family business. He had, Humphries wrote, the faintest stammer, implying 'a measure of sensitivity deeply and brutally submerged – as it always is, if ever present, in the Australian character' (a touch of Tid):

> I was in the Bank of New South Wales in Berkeley Square the other day, and I ran into Wally Sutcliffe. He wasn't at school but he's a helluva nice guy. He's just done the Continent and reckons Copenhagen takes some beating; had to drag himself away from all that lovely ice-cold Carlsberg. Apparently Italy gave him a touch of the toms; too commercialized altogether and you pay through the nose for everything. Not that old Wally's short of a bob, his parents are pretty well-lined finance-wise.

Buster thought that England was 'a fantastic place holiday-wise, but the beer's punk and you can't pull in as many notes – in my line of country – as you can back home. Fair enough?' A female variant, akin in philistine complacency, if not in drunkenness, is Debbie Thwaite of the same period: 'Mind you, I must admit there are compensations living in London. For instance, cheese is cheaper.'

Other pathetic and pushy expatriates now poured from Humphries' teeming imagination: Eric Ballaratë, a young tenor from Ballarat who had won the Lubra Oil Quest at home and is trying to make it at Covent Garden; Lantana Holman, an Australian art dealer who loathes his country-men; and Malcolm Foxcroft, an old and mediocre actor whose greatest moment was a chance encounter with D.H. Lawrence at a Sydney beach in 1922. None of these characters made stage or record. They reflected Humphries' early London experience and would later culminate in the adventures of Barry McKenzie. But for the moment they did not seem to lead anywhere.

For a natural performer who delights in publicity this was a barren and frustrating period, both in a still unimpressed London and in an Australia at least partly resentful of 'expatriates'. Any journalist from Melbourne who called on him seeking a story was sure of a welcome. 'Bullocks' hearts all right?' he asked one reporter, inviting him to lunch and assuming the mask of the Wild Colonial before switching to the Deep Melbourne Provincial to explain how far behind Melbourne London was culturally: 'There's no music bowl or drive-in picture shows. And we looked in vain for a barbecue or kiddies' play centre at Stratford-on-Avon'; or to complain about English ingratitude.

I'm also most disappointed to discover how few people express gratitude for the food parcels we sent during the war. I've only had one complaint, from a family who got a case of crystallized fruit and ate it all and became sick. I pointed out that we went without a lot to send all those tins of jam and cashew nuts. There's no gratitude in the world.

Then in the role of the Mad Collector he displayed his newly acquired first editions of neglected if not entirely unread *fin de siècle* romances – Marmaduke Pickthall's *Saïd the Fisherman*, Haldane MacFall's *The Wooings of Jezebel Pettyfer*, Count Stenbock's *Studies of Death* or Matthew Phipps Shiel's *Prince Zaleski*. Finally, as the Mad Composer, he announced the musical comedy he was just finishing:

> In the first act white Australians discover that the aboriginals are not a fading race at all. Secretly for years they've been building up numbers in caves and the outback. When they are strong enough they march on Melbourne and take it over.
>
> The second act opens at a white reservation in Central Australia, with aboriginals guarding the barbed wire compound and inside a group of representative Australians – Mr Menzies, Gladys Moncrieff, Lou Richards . . .

It was enough to guarantee him headlines back in Australia where it was an alternative to the published jibes which were swiftly posted over to London. Characteristic of these was the review in a Sydney magazine of Humphries' record 'Sandy Agonistes' by an Adelaide critic Max Harris: It had always been an open question, Harris began, 'whether Barry Humphrey [*sic*] would see the distance'. It was now clear that he was 'a flash in the pan'. His satires on London expatriates were 'thin' and 'profitless'.

> Those Australian girls, the physios, nurses and kindergartners, who cram together into an Australian huddle in pokey London flats, live more narrowly provincial lives in the heart of Empire than they do in Caulfield. This is not a complex point to make: nor is it devastatingly funny. Such lasses are more pathetic than funny, and it is hard to enjoy Humphrey [*sic*] employing a sub-machine gun on the flopsy bunnies.

The embittered Melbourne businessman included on the
record, Colin Cartwright, who has failed to buy his family's
affection, ('The wife's crying out for a liquidizer so I get her
one. Must have used it once in six months. Fifteen quid for a
glass of carrot juice. How's that!') was outside Humphries'
vocal capabilities – 'he is vocally no Peter Sellers or
O'Shaughnessy for that matter' – and was 'a dull piece of
social observation'. Humphries had become 'an obsessive
bore' ... 'a wandering bore' ... 'a proverbial party bore' ...
and (to make sure the point was not missed) 'like Milton, he
is on the side of the devil of boredom without knowing it'.

At this point, in 1961, Cliff Hocking of Melbourne came to
Humphries with a portentous idea that was to change
everything. Hocking was beginning his own spectacular
career as a theatrical entrepreneur, but his only show so far
had been an Australian tour by an Indian classical music
ensemble. He now proposed something Humphries had
never considered – a one-man show, featuring Edna and
Sandy. It would be a short 'off-Broadway' type of experi-
ment. It would also be a gamble since a one-man show
depends almost entirely on the actor's ability to involve the
audience, to bring it, in the words of Ruth Draper, 'up on to
the stage and into the scene with you'. Hocking was
confident that Humphries could do this: it was precisely
what he had been doing in the most successful scenes of the
Rock 'n' Reel Revue in Melbourne.

For his part Humphries' eagerness was tempered only by
his contract for *Oliver!*. Then, like Ko-Ko in *The Mikado*, he
was freed by a set of curious chances. As he put it: 'The
management wouldn't release me despite all sorts of pleas.
So after eighteen months I finally got a doctor to get me out
on medical grounds. I was having a sort of breakdown, so
they released me for a while. I made sure of things then by
accident. I went down to Cornwall to write my Australian
show that was coming up, went out for a walk near a river,

slipped on ice, and shot down this frozen water-race and over a precipice. I broke several things and lay there for a full day until I was rescued by what seemed to be the full cast of "The Pirates of Penzance".'

The press described it as 'one of the most dramatic rescues ever made in Britain' as the helicopter pilot could not find level ground on which to land and had to winch Humphries to safety.

'At least,' he concluded, 'I got released from *Oliver!*'

8

The One-Man Show Man

On a windy winter night, 30 July 1962, in a church hall in central Melbourne, Mrs Edna Everage sidled on to the stage to open *A Nice Night's Entertainment*, the first of the series of entertainments which over the coming thirty years would make Humphries the most popular one-man showman in the history of theatre. Dressed in a green pill-box hat and net (like Jackie Kennedy's), with a clashing red coat, pearls, earrings, gloves, corsage and butterfly spectacles with a touch of diamanté, she exclaimed 'Excuse I!' and began discussing her trip to the Old Country: 'We have no reason to fear overseas fashions. I visited all the big cities, and though I was from Australia, quite a few heads turned, I can tell you!' Then after singing a terrifying tribute to 'Australian Vitality' followed by an Anzac Day song (to a guffawing audience): 'Ours was a War Savings Street! Was *yours*? ... *Yours? Yours?*', she brought the audience up to date on her husband Norm, on her children Valmai, Kenny and Bruce and her travelling companion Madge ('We were broadened together'). She cast her basilisk eye over Australian architecture, fashion and food (recommending French cutlets *anglaise* at a Woolworth's gourmette and offering her recipe for tomato sauce: to 20 lb of tomatoes, add ¼ gallon vinegar and 10 oz salt) and ended the first act by complimenting Prime Minister Menzies on his remark that Australia is becoming a melting-pot. 'It's just a question of who's going to melt first ...' she said, pausing, then shrieking: 'It won't be me!' It was the most successful so far of all Edna Everage's appearances in Melbourne.

Before she returned in the second act, Sandy Stone, seated in pyjamas and dressing gown in his dimly spotlit moth-eaten armchair, presented, 'Can You Keep a Secret?', his longest and most complex sketch yet. If, in the 1950s, Humphries' stress was on Sandy's suburban drabness (with touches of poetry), in the 1960s Sandy, while still sad and sexless, becomes increasingly kindly, stoic and elegiac. Now he tells of his and Beryl's ordeal in looking after the neighbour's children, Wayne and Marilyn, over Easter. (For generations most of the Stone line have been 'without issue', as are Sandy and Beryl.) The experience was so exhausting that when it was over, 'I forgot to put the [rubbish] tins out' and Beryl 'got quite weepy'. Sandy then acted out the old nursery game:

> Can you keep a secret?
> I don't suppose you can.
> You mustn't laugh
> You musn't cry
> But do the best you can.

Mrs Everage then stormed back ('Let me look at you ... you haven't changed a bit') to show some of her 'four million', then voguish, colour slides of her Trip (the Indian Ocean through a deck-rail; rubbish dumps in Aden; Buckingham Palace: 'That's where SHE lives. You can't see her but she looked RADIANT!') She also reported with pride (to the distress of one critic) that she had joined in the trendy Aldermaston Ban-the-Bomb March (along with Barry Humphries). But most significantly she began her infamous habit of saying the unsayable – this time the unsayable anti-Catholicism of a largely Protestant audience: describing her son's new house, the view from which is obscured by a

Catholic convent on the top of a hill, she remarked with prim bigotry and a rising stridency: 'There's no doubt about them, is there? They always pick the best positions!' The audience was both aghast and relieved to hear, publicly paraded, one of Protestant Australia's most cherished resentments. There had been nothing like this on the Australian stage before and it was Humphries' loudest laugh yet – and another sign of things to come.

The show also paraded other characters from Humphries' expanding repertoire – the Mad Scientist as a black-coated, homburg-hatted Minister for National Identity charged with the responsibility of imposing an Australian uniformity on his countrymen, including a regulation, ultra-violet sun-tan by subcutaneous injections and the compulsory nasal twang by 'immobilizing the tongue' with an Ausmophone fitted to the throat. ('Soon no individual can leave this country without having first passed through our hands and been scientifically, and if necessary surgically, invested with the official Oz image.') There was an embittered provincial journalist with an all too recognizable prototype, who envied and hated successful Australian expatriates, and read his open letter to Joan Sutherland, 'Sorry Joan, You've Lost Your Touch':

> I'm not just getting at you Joan. The same goes for all your ex-Australian mates, and you'll do them a favour if you pass this around.
>
>   ... I hope you're having a ball fellas; it cost you enough to get there didn't it ... a little item called *talent*, remember? The sad fact is, you're all on the skids, and have been since you turned your back on Australia and went after the bright lights and the facile acclamation of a bunch of snobs. You might fool them in England, but you can't pull the wool over our eyes back in Australia.
>
> If any of you members of the so-called 'Australian colony' deign to pay us a visit some time (and it may

surprise you to learn that we don't much care whether you do or not), don't expect the red carpet ... you might even get the raspberry! And if you think we're going to bribe you to come home with astrological salaries, you've got another think coming. Sopranos are tuppence a dozen, and there are plenty of people at home to paint our pictures for us. We don't want scum like you who've got to be paid to visit their homeland. We don't want people who've spent the last few years of their lives at plushy Chelsea parties knocking their mates back home and ratting on Australia. Don't think we haven't got you taped; don't think we've forgotten you ...

You're a bunch of bloody traitors! Rats, Rats, RATS!'

Addressing the audience, he concluded: 'You may wonder why I feel so deeply about all this. Why I feel it is my duty to expose all these unfortunate people. You see, they all happen to be personal friends of mine'.

There was also Morrie Tate, the guitar-toting beatnik in black duffel-coat, stove-pipe jeans and Roman sandals, who picked his nose in silence for five minutes before singing this parody of autobiography:

> I was then twenty-two and Sandra eighteen
> We lived on cheese, yoghurt and Dexedrine;
> Man, I really got jack of like nobody has
> The Human Predicament and all that jazz.
>
> I don't want to write and I don't want to teach,
> Just hitch up to Sydney and sleep on the beach;
> I'm living for kicks man, I live off my wits,
> And surburban conformity gives me the shits.

Intending at this time only to test the market, Cliff Hocking had booked the show for a few nights only in small halls in the main cities, but so great was the public response that it could have run for weeks. The critics were almost unanimous. Roger Covell of the *Sydney Morning Herald* called Humphries 'the most original entertainer at large in Australia', while Geoffrey Hutton of the Melbourne *Age* described him as both funny and lethal, 'as nice as a tiger snake'. Only the Sydney *Daily Telegraph*'s Denis O'Brien found a 'humour too private for mass Sydney', a show 'too long' and an appeal limited to a 'coterie'.

Soon afterwards Barry Humphries made his début in New York, playing Mr Sowerberry (and sometimes Fagin) at the Imperial Theater on West 55th Street. It was the winter of early 1963 and from a cold-water flat in West 10th Street he responded at once to the charm of Greenwich Village – then still a 'rather sedate neighbourhood', hospitable to many minorities, ethnic, cultural and sexual. 'A lot of people I knew had lived there for years: old booze-ravaged Bohemians washed up from the thirties, and second-hand booksellers who had actually known the authors whose works they purveyed. There were famous jazz cellars, pioneer health-food shops and bespoke sandal-makers who did a roaring trade in that carefree interlude between the beatniks and hippies.' He met the Dada guru Carl Van Vechten, the Dada artist Marcel Duchamp, and the one-time surrealist Salvador Dali (whose wife cut his hair), but above all he met the beatnik novelist Jack Kerouac, whose tales of sentimental and shiftless waifs and bar-flies he had waded through when working up the itinerant guitarist Morrie Tate for his first one-man show. Humphries already found Kerouac's characters unworthy of the robust tradition of Whitman and Thoreau (and his scepticism deepened as the decade progressed), but in 1963 he clicked with their creator and he met him each night after the show at a bar called The Ninth Circle. 'How's our English poet tonight?' Kerouac would inquire, offering a drink and always refusing to accept that Humphries was an Australian actor.

One winter night Kerouac threw a party in an enormous

black furniture van into which the customers from The Ninth Circle climbed with their booze, paraffin lamps, candles, guitars, cigarettes, girlfriends and peanuts. 'In a flurry of snowflakes, the hatch slammed shut. The author of *On the Road* thumped the driver's window, the huge vehicle tiptoed into the night and our party began its stately progress through the snowbound streets of Manhattan . . .'

Something of Barry Humphries lingers in that huge, ghostly black van . . . the Bunyip in him, the Tid, the Estragon, the Sandy Stone, the Papageno who is never entirely silenced by the shrieking of Dame Edna or the belching of Sir Les.

On returning to London, Humphries made the first of his two unsuccessful attempts in the 1960s to exhibit his Aussie characters on the London stage. It was in May 1963 at the Establishment Club where Peter Cook had asked Humphries to fill in for the American Lenny Bruce when the British authorities refused to allow that 'obscene drug addict' to do an English tour. Dame Edna's 1989 autobiography, *My Gorgeous Life*, gives an ironic eye-witness account of the fiasco. As she arrived at the Establishment she was greeted by a tall willowy young man in a charcoal-grey suit 'who had the boyish habit of inclining his head to one side, looking down his long nose and flicking back a light brown forelock'. He had 'a little upside-down smile, like a thin, kind shark'. It was Peter Cook. Inside, some university students were doing impersonations of Harold Macmillan and stopping a bit to laugh at themselves and light smelly cigarettes. Then Barry Humphries began 'his endless chatter':

That evening the little tables in the club were packed with celebrities, and kind, supportive Peter pointed some of them out to me as we nibbled our steaks in the corner. That jolly little balding man with the wavy upper lip was

John Betjeman, the famous poet, who apparently adored me. Over there in a grubby pink suit was a droopy man whose arms were too long for his body, chain smoking cigarettes with the wrong fingers. His name was Tynan, a critic apparently, and I blushed to think he had the same Christian name as my own manly little son. Jean Shrimpton, the famous glamour-puss, was looking bewildered. Holding forth at her table was a carrot-headed, camel-faced man in a crumpled corduroy suit called Dr Miller, who seemed to be trying to knot his arms together with some degree of success. I even noticed a few journalists with notebooks at the ready.

But where, she asked, as Humphries droned on and on, were 'the bursts of laughter' which used to sometimes interrupt his shows in Australia? 'Instead of laughter and the splatter of applause, I could hear an odd shuffling and clattering noise and even the sound of people chatting quite loudly amongst themselves.'

Humphries also converted the Minister for National Identity from his one-man show of 1962 into an immigration official based at Australia House. 'Lank, dirt-coloured lady-length hair flapping across his face,' the *Daily Mail* reported, 'his eyes tiny like diamond chips, his mouth slit and thin like a beak, Barry Humphries looked for all the world like an emu in moult.' He had this to say to the unresponsive audience at the Establishment:

I've never been to Australia, but I'd like to clear up any wrong impressions.

Of course, it's easy for you to see for yourselves. We've got our roving press gangs – er, mobile immigration units – out and about.

Or you've only got to have a tenner and you can walk into the jaws – er, doors – of Australia House, whisper the word 'immigration' and be whisked by chute into our 'pre-assimilation clinic' where your skin will be tanned and your tongue immobilized to give you the correct national accent. I then offer you the hand-stitched scrotum of an old-man kangaroo chock-a-block with a delicious assortment of Australian dried fruit, followed by an astringent glass of Emu wine, or should you prefer it, a balloon of Foster's lager.

You may think your Englishness will count against you in Australia.

It will.

For her part, Mrs Everage, with a Qantas bag over one shoulder and a spray of wattle on her lapel, confided to the few remaining listeners:

You have so much tradition here. It's so wonderful we hardly notice your low standard of living ... We sent you food parcels during the war. We put up with the rationing and sometimes we could only have meat once a day ...

As for those who say the English don't bath enough – I always say it would be a funny world if we all smelt the same, now wouldn't it?

Then she shook hands with a West Indian: 'It's so nice to meet a typical Londoner.'

But the act was a flop and the critics were as discouraging as the chattering audiences. Julian Holland in the *Daily Mail* thought Humphries lacked 'anger' and Bamber Gascoigne in the *Spectator* found his characters 'distinctly soporific'. The act was soon dropped and Humphries later referred to his 'highly successful, five-minute season' at the Establishment. It confirmed his conviction that his Aussie characters would never be accepted on the English stage.

9

Just a Show

In 1964 the Humphries moved into an unfurnished flat in a Georgian house at 25 Maida Avenue, London W2. The roof leaked and there were squatters downstairs but it was in the heart of Little Venice, on the banks of the Regent's Park canal and within a few minutes' drive of Hyde Park and Park Lane. In time the squatters left, the building was repaired and the Humphries filled the spacious and high-ceilinged rooms with their period furniture, their paintings, prints and bric-à-brac. Humphries had brought a Melbourne GPO turn-of-the-century brass telephone with him and had picked up a huge plaster statue of Ariadne by Alfred Gilbert, the sculptor who did Eros in Piccadilly Circus. There was also a collection of signed Galle glass, an Erard grand piano and a tall abstract fibre-glass sculpture by the Australian Michael Kellaway.

One reporter, R.J. Scholfield, who visited Humphries at this time sketched a vignette of settled domestic bliss:

> There he benevolently rules a household consisting of fair-haired New Zealand wife Rosalind, daughters Tessa, twenty months, and Emily, six weeks, and a French *au pair*, Dominique. The drawing room, with its air of decadent Edwardian luxury, might have been designed as a fortress against Mrs Everage. The walls are crowded with designs by Charles Conder depicting the lesbian boudoirs

of Balzac's novels, bulgy creatures lolling and entwined, like bundles of worms. The theme extends to two large sour dolls from the Caledonian Market that glare from the top of the grand piano, where they sit with their arms stiffly around each other.

Squeezed between the lesbians are other paintings by Tom Roberts, Holman Hunt, Arthur Boyd and Abraham Louis Buvelot. On the lavatory wall hangs a sketch of Humphries' old school, Melbourne Grammar. The donor of this work was John Betjeman, who picked it up in a junk shop.

He makes a good living in London, and although he could probably earn more in Australia in the short term his range of performance there would be more limited.

If the theme of settled domesticity was to prove to be illusory, the note of confident artistic success was surer. Barry Humphries was now beginning to be in demand in London, although still in small parts in musicals, comedies and pantos. In 1963 he played Captain Jules Martin in *The Bed-Sitting Room* by John Antrobus and Spike Milligan at the Duke of York's, St Martin's Lane, and Heinrich, the Mad Scientist, in Peter Shaffer's *The Merry Rooster's Panto* at Wyndham's, Charing Cross Road. In 1964 he played the ear-splitting balladeer in Lionel Bart's *Maggie May* at the Adelphi in the Strand, opening and closing the show, leaving him free to visit other shows in between – at one of which Spike Milligan so 'spiked' his drink that he almost slept through his final appearance, arriving on stage at the last second to end the show in his street clothes and without his drum and cymbals. On another occasion, he returned to the stage at the wrong theatre. 'It was a Joan Littlewood production, so it didn't matter.' (Humphries said later that the 1960s was a hazy period, in which he had many amusing and many devastating experiences, and some which 'I have no recollection of at all'.)

But his triumph of 1964 was his portrayal of the several
roles (Nun, Policeman, Old Lag, Greek Kayf-keeper, Lord
Sexkilling) in Joan Littlewood's production of Frank Nor-
man's *A Kayf up West* at the Theatre Royal, Stratford East.
Bamber Gascoigne now found his performances the 'main
pleasure' of the show; Ronald Bryden noted his 'dazzling
displays of versatility' and Hugh Leonard wrote: 'The best
performance was that of Barry Humphries whose wicked
ogling of the audience during his brief appearance as a nun
was the best thing of the evening, although one remembers
his Lord Sexkilling and his café owner with affection.' In
1964 he also launched the *Private Eye* career of Barry
McKenzie, began compiling *Bizarre*, his first anthology of
curiosa, and prepared a new one-man show, *Excuse I*, for his
Australian tour of 1965.

It was a triumphant return to Australia. There could no
longer be any suggestion of mere 'coterie appeal' as he filled
huge theatres for weeks on end, filling the gods for the first
time since the hey-day of the famous Australian vaudevil-
lean, Mo (Roy Rene). No one-man show had ever done such
business in Australia; the other one-man show at the same
time, Marlene Dietrich's, pulled smaller houses, to the
chagrin and amazement of 'the Firm', the theatrical entrepreneur, J.C. Williamson, which had cut Humphries' seasons
short to make room for the great *chanteuse*. (He did return
seasons.)

Humphries' main Aussie characters were again Edna and
Sandy. By now Edna was moving more firmly with the
times, planting avocado seeds, making pasta (which she
dried out on her rotary clothes hoist), and simply 'adoring'
satire and yoga. She also ridiculed public figures and
celebrities more freely: since Joan Sutherland had concluded
a tumultuous curtain-call by singing 'Home Sweet Home',
so did Edna, with a frightening exuberance – setting a
pattern for her future parodies of the *glitterati* of stage and

screen. Above all, in 1965 she introduced the hurling of 'gladdies' at the audience in the *finale*: it began originally in Adelaide before the Christmas shut-down as a way of disposing of surplus flowers. The audience was made to hold them up, quiver them and join in community singing. It was an enormously popular innovation and became the traditional *finale* of the shows, ultimately requiring over a hundred bunches, sometimes imported from Sicily or South Africa and kept warmed and watered in a special room. It also involved the audience, almost totally, in Edna's world: it was now impossible to laugh patronizingly at her from a great distance.

This time the occasion for the Sandy Stone sketch ('Sandy Claus') was not Easter, but Christmas, and the Stones' midday dinner for a few friends. The turkey was served on Beryl's best crockery with her 'Cries of London' dinner mats, and after the pudding all listened to the Queen's speech and the bushfire warnings. That night a hot wind carried someone's laughter through the neighbourhood and rattled the venetians. Beryl cried and rambled in her sleep, but next morning she said she had slept like a log and told Sandy not to talk a lot of twaddle. He concluded: 'It's funny though, isn't it, the way you can't remember your dreams?'

Other characters in the show included a beach bum (Nipper Dixon) who, after hammering Squeaky Hudson's drinking truck up the coast for the surf, 'demolishing a twelve' (-gallon keg of beer) with his mates, and rolling a few queers in Hyde Park ('You cannot beat the great Australian outdoor life') burst into his 'chundering' or vomiting song, to the tune of 'Maggie May':

> I've had liquid laughs in bars
> And I've hurled from moving cars
> And I've chuckled when and where it suited me.
> But if I could choose a spot
> To regurgitate me lot
> Then I'd chunder in the old Pacific sea.

Drink it up. Drink it up.
Crack another dozen tubes and prawns with me.
If you want to throw your voice,
Mate, you don't have any choice
But to chunder in the old Pacific sea.

A kindred spirit of the same period was an unnamed skier
who would now be called a yuppie, and whose song is to the
tune of 'Good King Wenceslas':

Bring me gluhwein, bring me beer
And a crate of ice-cold tinnies.
Off we hammer every year
In our Volksies and our Minis.
In some cosy Alpine spot
There you're sure to find us,
Propelling Charlies to the cot
With a queue of blokes behind us.

(As editor of the *Bulletin* magazine at this time, I arranged
for a record to be made of the surfing and skiing songs from
the show and the record was a hit and quickly sold out.)

There was also another Mad Scientist (Dodd, a Public
Relations guru and manipulator of the masses), and a trendy,
tortured intellectual, Neil Singleton – the culmination of
Humphries' earlier spoofs of pretentiousness and the harbinger of the series of larger-than-life cultural frauds of his later
shows.

The critics joined the public in its delight at seeing
Australia in a fresh light, sometimes even seeing it for
the first time at all. One critic (Mungo McCallum Jr)
suggested that Humphries might be the funniest man in the
world. If Elijah Moshinsky discerned a certain nihilism in the
show, it was, he said, a hilarious nihilism. Even the Sydney
Daily Telegraph conceded that the 1965 show was sturdier

than the one it had dismissed as coterie stuff in 1962, and
only the simultaneous publication of Humphries' salmagundi
of freaks, *Bizarre*, with its 'sick smell' (*Sydney Morning
Herald*), gave the butts of his satire some fuel for counter-
attack.

In any case, back in London Barry Humphries increased
his frenetic, almost demonic, pace. His friend, the comic
writer John Wells, has referred to Humphries' 'almost insane
rage' at this period. He was appearing with Wells, and
Eleanor Bron, Will Rushton and Malcolm Muggeridge, in
the BBC television's *The Late Late Show*, produced by Hugh
Burnett in 1966 and Jack Gold in 1967, and continued to be
dissatisfied with the roles he was given. He knew, he told
Wells, that there were some things he was really very good
at, but he had no opportunity, he believed, to show them.
Did I go to the wrong university? he asked. At least the show
allowed him to introduce Mrs Everage regularly to comparatively large audiences. (So urgent was Humphries' hunger
for public recognition at this time that, according to Wells,
he was heard hissing in the ear of a taxi-driver he was paying
off in the presence of others beginning to make their names
in television: 'Five shillings? Ten bob if you say "Thank you,
Barry".')

In 1967, a year in which 'I missed only four days' work,' he
had his first film role in Peter Cook and Dudley Moore's
movie *Bedazzled*, playing the sin of Envy, 'a perfect role for
any Australian actor'. He also played Fagin for six months in
Oliver! at the Piccadilly: 'I played him as Edna Everage with
a beard' – and from time to time ad-libbed a line, as when
after the Six Day War in Israel, the sound of a nearby
explosive bang evoked Fagin's comment: 'Arabs?' (the sort
of joke discouraged by Lionel Bart). At Christmas, following
Sir Bernard Miles and Sir Donald Wolfit in the role, he
played Long John Silver in *Treasure Island* at the Mermaid.
('I am the first commoner to play him. Weeks on end being
pecked to death by Bernard Miles' parrot!') Long John Silver

was his best received role since his trio of parts in *Kayf*: Michael Billington remarked on his 'enormous gusto' and on how his eyes 'roll around in their sockets like silver balls in a puzzle-box'. At the same time he prepared *The Barry Humphries Book of Innocent Austral Verse* and began refining the new sad-funny grotesques and frauds that would join Edna and Sandy in his next entertainment, *Just a Show* of 1968 – which, if it were as successful in Australia as the 1965 *Excuse I* had been, he would bring to London and finally lay the ghost of his flop at the Establishment in 1963.

Edna Everage was now abandoning her suburban-dowdy appearance. As captured in a painting at this time by John Brack, Edna, smiling like a shark, was a gaudy mess of clashing colours, from a shapeless blue floral hat, pink diamanté glasses, a heavy pearl choker, red Thai silk coat over a green dress, down to low-heeled pumps with pom-poms ('Am I over-dressed?' she asked, staring about her. 'No, I don't think so.') The other 1968 innovation was Edna's entry from the stalls chatting with her audience, her 'possums'. She was now becoming the hostess of a theatre party and her vitriolic give-and-take with the audience became an Everage hallmark, along with the gladdie-trembling *finale* and constant touches of zaniness: 'Get off the phone, you dirty pervert!' she shouted in support of Madge Allsop, who was being troubled in Adelaide by a breather; but the caller was Edna's husband Norm, ringing from Melbourne. She also sang 'Edna's Hymn' of a golden, lost Australia, in a mood of nostalgia which the increasingly forward-looking Edna was soon to lose:

Australia is a Saturday with races on the tranny,
Australia is the talcy smell of someone else's Granny;
Australia is a kiddy with zinc creme on its nose,
Australia is my mother's pair of pink supportive hose;
Australia's famous postage stamps are stuffed with flowers
  and fauna,
Australia is the Little Man who's open round the corner;

Australia is a sunburnt land, of sand and surf and snow —
All ye who do not love her
Ye know where ye can go!

In his 1968 sketch Sandy Stone is in hospital recovering from
his op and recalling the grand old days of the tennis club
before the war. Beryl used to be 'a little humdinger in the
mixed doubles ... it always seems afternoon when you're
playing mixed doubles'. Once they won the Lucky Spot at a
dance and a pound box of chocolates. He is worried
(pointlessly as it would turn out) about Beryl's loneliness if
he should die first. 'It was different in the old days ... But
you can't win the lucky spot all your life.'

Other characters in the show included Brian Graham, a
brisk blond Sydney mining executive, in navy blue shorts
and long white socks, who nurses a guilty secret – as for the
first time on the Australian stage a homosexual is sympathe-
tically presented. Always on the telephone, he is in turn a
high-tech phosphate salesman; a punching bag for a bullying
father; a flirt with a homosexual friend's wife; and a mincing
bitchy queer – until under the stress of living out so many
roles he breaks down. His last moving words, to his
suspicious father, are: 'I am alone'.

Although the possibility of a crack-up, mental or physical
– the Tid factor – is always hovering in the background of
Humphries' driven young men, Brian Graham is the only
character to undergo one: the rest are irrepressible.

The folk singer of the show was Big Sonia in a long black
wig and a microskirt as well as Roman sandals. She wants to
go to Vietnam, talk to the Viet Cong and sing to them and
our boys together: 'I don't have to tell you what the bosses
said to that. That's right, no!' In any case she has enough big
bookings at protest rallies. She finishes with her song:

I sing a song of suffering
Of agony and pain

> And if you haven't suffered
> I'll sing my song again.

An innovation of the 1968 show was the introduction of film and an 'underground' film-maker or *auteur*, Martin Agrippa, who had been experimenting with the revolutionary Blind Man's Cinema and whose 'The End' had won the coveted Bronzed Scrotum in Helsinki:

A lot of kids who were close to me while this film was being made knew something bloody meaningful was happening, and I guess I did too in a curious kind of way. The story kind of happened like the best modern jazz music. I just took myself off to Bilgola Beach with a tape recorder and talked. God how I talked! I talked about my childhood, my attitudes to my parents, to women, my responses to hallucinatory drugs, to the finest in modern jazz music and towards the place of creative people such as myself in antipodean society – I even talked about myself.

I talked about the colour syndrome and the Aboriginal bit in Australian life, and I talked about the hateful incubus of censorship blighting the cultural expression of our young poets, film-makers and jazz musicians.

I talked of images too; The surfrider poised on a green wall of water, the curious spendour of old-age pensioners eating, the flawless phrasing of the late Charles Parker, the ageless symmetry of an egg, the statuesque beauty of a newborn child, and the timeless quality of my own reflection in the eyes of Yvette Lumsden. I poured all of myself, of my consciousness and creativity, into those reels and reels of tape in the house at Bilgola Beach, and those tapes have been distilled into the motion picture you are about to see.

This isn't a pretty film. It's crude and rough and instinctual. As crude and rough and instinctual as the

Australian landscape itself. It isn't a nice cosy motion picture made by nice, cosy, sold-out professionals. But is the universe cosy? Is God a professional?

The short film shown was in fact made by the Australian director Bruce Beresford, then Secretary of the British Film Institute Production Board. He made it at his house in Brixton, using a Nigerian to play an Australian Aborigine and filming a scene of a girl rushing naked through the bush in a park in Highgate. It cost £200. 'People who see it,' Beresford said, 'think it is a genuine experimental movie. It is completely bogus! The hard thing was making it bad enough' – by deliberately scratching the negative or making the splices jumpy. When it was later shown, to acclaim, at a European festival of 'underground' cinema, no one saw the joke.

Just a Show also presented the businessman, Rex Lear, a foul-mouthed drunk who collapses at his ungrateful daughter's wedding breakfast (on 17 February, Humphries' birthday), insults the head waiter ('I know all about you dagos. You don't know the first thing about family life as we know it in Australia') and vomits into a potted palm. It was an extraordinary *tour-de-force* as Humphries, single-handed, played father, bridesmaid, vicar, best man, caterer and waiter.

The show repeated the success of 1965 with both critics and public. Geoffrey Hutton said it was 'his funniest performance since his pioneering days'; Katherine Brisbane 'regretted the evening coming to an end'; and H.G. Kippax noted a rousing, roof-raising popular success. Some were offended by Rex Lear's drunken obscenities but Humphries insisted: 'I don't compromise in what I write or in the way my characters speak.' The Australian public was becoming increasingly engaged not only in Sandy's gloom and Edna's mania but, through the other characters, in Humphries' rage. He was accepted as Australia's most creative stage writer and the progenitor of a new wave of vernacular dramatists (committing the offence, as he put it, of ante-plagiarism).

The Australian success of *Just a Show* confirmed Humphries in his decision to make his second attempt in the 1960s to present his characters on the London stage at the small West End Fortune Theatre. The attempt was again unsuccessful. Also called *Just a Show*, it was substantially the same as the Australian version. But the critics were almost unanimous. Harold Hobson dismissed it in one devastating sentence: 'Most of Barry Humphries' *Just a Show* will give pleasure to most Australians in London.' Irving Wardle thought Humphries 'a limited performer' and Benedict Nightingale saw little more than 'a good mimic'.

There was one qualification to this dismissal – a general delight in Edna's gladdie-waving *finale*. Hilary Spurling said it was 'one of those unforgettable moments in the theatre', Julian Jebb called it 'one of the strangest and funniest quarters of an hour you could spend inside a theatre', B.A. Young thought it was 'funnier than anything I remember for a long time'; and Herbert Kretzner wrote: 'The mood of those [last] ten minutes cannot be produced in words. It was one of those magic moments in the theatre where the audience becomes truly happy.' If Jeremy Kingston caught the public mood when he lamented: 'theatres won't let you in for just the last quarter of an hour', it was at least now clear in what direction Barry Humphries would ultimately move.

But meanwhile the rest of the Humphriesian family was continuing to grow, a whole gallery of intellectual pseuds, various manifestations of Mad Dr Humphries the Raving Ratbag, and above all Barry McKenzie . . . .

10

The Adventures of Bazza McKenzie

A characteristic Humphriesian figure of the 1960s is the hobbledehoy – young, awkward, unpretentious and often drunk. Buster Thompson, the pub-crawling tourist from Melbourne, and Nipper Dixon, the chundering surfie from Sydney are early examples – the first on record only, the second on both stage and record. But the greatest and most enduring of Humphries' hobbledoys was Barry or Bazza McKenzie who has never appeared on stage or record (although he starred in two films) and who first emerged as a comic-strip character in *Private Eye* magazine on 10 July 1964 as 'Barry McKensie [*sic*]. Australian at large.' Peter Cook suggested the strip to Humphries after hearing Buster Thompson on record, and Nicholas Garland created Bazza's appearance after watching an Anzac Day service in London.

Bazza was more plebeian (more Sydney) than Buster and, while he did not have Buster's faint stammer, he had a different set of inhibitions: this amiable, invincible provincial in a double-breasted suit with baggy trousers, striped tie and broad-brimmed hat, this boozing, vomiting, urinating, randy Australian was also a genteel puritan, terrified of women and poofters, although he concealed his terror behind an engaging colonial bravura:

> One day I strode
> Down the Earl's Court Road,

When into a pub I was lured.
'Where are you from?'
Asked a nosey Pom,
As I downed the amber fluid.
'I'll tell you straight,
I'm Australian mate,
And I feel like getting plastered.
But the beer's crook,
And the girls all look
Like you – you Pommy Bastard!

A colonial Candide in an Akubra hat, he and his oafish mates
blundered through the Swinging England of the 1960s –
with its doomed flower people, its double-dealing folk
singers, trendy TV producers, thieving porters, cheating
taxi-drivers, dotty (and always pregnant) potters, necrophi-
liac undertakers, crazy Jewish psychiatrists, rorting Aussie
dentists, lesbian nurses – in a picaresque series of adventures,
always enlivened by his exuberant vernacular, a guide to
which was published as an appendix to the second book of
the strip, *Bazza Pulls It Off* (and also distributed separately at
the Bazza movies.) Here is a selection:

bastard. A nice person.
big smoke, the. A metropolis (like Melbourne or Paris).
big spit, to go the. To hurl, chunder or play the whale.
bonzer (see under *whacko-the-diddle-oh*. Beaut, extra grouse
and fan-bloody-tastic.
brewer's droop. Alcoholically induced impotence.
brick short of a load. Simple-minded.
Captain Cook, to take a. To take a dekko, to look.
chilled ones (chilled glass) (see under *foaming frosties, neck
oil, stubbies, coldies, Fosters*). Lager beer.
Chuck, enough to make you (see under *chunder, technico-
lor yawn, hurl, play the whale, park the tiger, cry Ruth*).
chunder, to. See above. To cry Ruth, Herb or Bert. To
enjoy oneself in reverse.

coo-ee. A universal Australian form of greeting.

drain, to (see under *point percy, syphon the python, strain the potatoes, water the horses, wring the rattlesnake, shake hands with the unemployed, slash,* etc). To micturate.

dunny (see under *throttling pit, slash house, thunder box*). bathroom, W.C., phone booth.

exercise the ferret, to (see under *dip the wick*).

jack of, to be. To be weary of.

jeez (see under *cripes*).

jerkin' the gherkin. Stropping the mulligan, rod walloping, twanging the wire.

John Bull (see under *schicker*, plastered). Intoxicated, full (as a state school).

John Thomas (see under *wick, ferret, mutton, beef bayonet, beef bugle, sausage, pencil, donger, unemployed, fat, gherkin, mulligan, snorker, tummy banana, percy*). Wife's best friend.

Mrs Palm and her five daughters (see under *jerkin' the gherkin*). A metaphor for the hand in all probability.

naughty, to have a. To dip the wick or to feature.

neck oil. Alcohol.

Ned Kelly whisky. An internationally recommended Australian beverage.

Oz. Australia.

Pat Malone, to be on one's. To be alone.

petrols, petrol bowsers. Trousers.

piss artist (see under *drop of the hard stuff, schicker*). A person given to habits of intemperance.

point percy, to (at the porcelain). To drain the dragon.

pom (syn, pommy bastard). English person.

potato peeler. Sheilah.

Qantas hostie. A desirable sexual partner.

shit a brick (see under *stone the crows, jeez, cripes, hack, starve the lizards*). A popular Australian exclamation of surprise.

skinful, to have a. To be replete with alcohol.

trouser snake, one-eyed (see under *ferret, John Thomas,* etc.)

wring the rattlesnake, to (see under *drain the dragon,* etc.)

xenophobia. A love of Australia.

The perennial theme in all his adventures is his endless search for – and, simultaneously, the evasion of – a sexual partner. 'When will our hero ever get his oats?' wrote in one desperate fan. Humphries replied:

He has been close. It's been handed to him on a plate on more than one occasion but he has shrunk from the brazen hussy:

a) because he was suddenly thirsty.

b) because he might cop a dose.

c) because she turned out to be an Australian with nice trusting aunties waiting back home and cherishing fantasies about her honour.

d) because he was suddenly shagged out.

e) because he didn't recognize the invitation or misconstrued it.

f) because he was full as a bull's bum or a prey to Brewer's Droop.

g) she probably wouldn't have liked it plain and simple.

These, and other reasons more arcane, inhibit our hero from getting the dirty water off his chest – to employ that most mysterious of all vernaculars for venereal relief. Barry constantly, obsessively, admits to carnal desire and he is swift to detect lubricity in the ladies he encounters, even when the reader might feel this imputation to be grossly misplaced. It is just that he baulks at a sexual dénouement.

Immediately a cult figure, Bazza was the first Humphries character to catch on in England – at a time when Edna, let alone Sandy, still left English audiences unmoved. For some it was almost as chic to find amusement in Bazza's scatological euphemisms as to find merit in the novels of, say, Amanda McKittrick Ros. Humphries himself launched this vogue in *The Times Literary Supplement* soon after the strip started, when, playing the role of Mad Dr Humphries, he airily referred to its 'superficial resemblance to the paintings of Teniers and his school' in seventeenth-century Flanders. (That is, in its scenes of urinating and vomiting.) John Wells was, however, probably the most successful with this ploy: he was particularly taken with the scene where Bazza, on a cross-Channel ferry, vomits over a lady and her chihuahua; apologetically wipes her down; picks up with his finger-tips the almost drowned little skin-and-bones dog and remarks 'Shit!!! I don't remember eating that.' Wells, with an irony equal to Humphries', described the incident as a 'luminous moment of rejection of European society', and declared that it 'must equal anything in Proust or André Gide'.

In 1968 the Australian Customs Department declared the book, *Bazza Pulls It Off*, a Prohibited Import (and disallowed the publisher's appeal against the decision). Humphries clowned for the press. Slumped in a chair, he murmured: 'Think what this will do to my reputation as someone the whole family can enjoy. It's a national disgrace – worse than a thrip plague, almost as bad as taxation.' Then, springing from his chair: 'But just between you and me, and I know you'll treat this confidentially, I'm ecstatic with pleasure. After all, this business will considerably enhance the subterranean value of the book.'

Warming to his theme (and the publicity), Humphries shovelled ridicule on the censorship authorities:

> Presumably the Customs bloke who read it must now be depraved and I feel that it's my fault. They will have to get in a new, wholesome man now to take his place. Really, the turnover in staff they must have there – a mind-

snapping concept. It would surely bring up the question of what happens to these people after they become depraved. I would hope the government provides properly for them. It would be interesting to know how long it takes for depravity to set in. Would the little woman have noticed anything bizarre about his behaviour when he came home that evening? After all, to read my book would have meant an hour's contact with unadulterated depravity. That is quite enough to corrupt him completely.

If his wife would like to contact me discreetly I might be able to help her with some of her new personal problems. Actually, I'm rather concerned about the legal aspects of all this. What are my obligations? . . . He couldn't sue me for loss of income now that his newfound depravity has cost him his job, could he?

As for myself, I have learnt to come to terms with my own gross depravity. The doctor has explained my condition to the wife and kids and they, too, have learnt to live with it.

But such has been my concern that I have recently inaugurated a society called Depravity Anonymous. The society is, as yet, in its infancy and so far has an all-male membership. Of course these facts might not concern the Minister any longer in view of the form his depravity has probably taken.

When, after a Court appeal and widespread protest, the Customs authorities began to consider lifting the ban on the book, Humphries implored them not to. 'The book is worthless from a literary point of view,' he insisted, 'and it is essential to the publicity for the film that the book remain banned in Australia for as long as possible.'

'I am employing a London public relations and publicity firm,' Humphries wrote to the Minister for Customs and Excise, 'to handle all press releases relating to this venture and they are naturally keen to hang their major story on the censorship situation in Australia. I do not feel that the photograph of yourself which they intend circulating does you complete justice and you may like to let us have one of your own choosing. In extending this courtesy to you I hope to reciprocate, in some small measure, your own great kindness in co-operating with me in banning my book, and assisting me in a formidable, and highly profitable, publicity campaign.

I remain sir,

Your Obedient Servant.'

When in due course the unfeeling Customs authorities released the book (before the opening of the first Bazza movie, financed by the same government that had banned the strip) some of the reviewers shared Humphries' opinion of its literary value: 'an insult to humanity', wrote one, and 'don't buy it!' advised another in a leading daily newspaper. Most however welcomed the book to the market: Max Harris managed to describe it as 'the best we've had in Australian black and white history.' The whole episode was one of the last writhings in Australia of the shortly to be abolished government censorship of books.

In *Private Eye* the strip ran for ten years (with interruptions) until, by March 1974, Humphries had characteristically pushed his editor's, Richard Ingrams', legendary patience to its limit, and after various scenes of gross lechery, perversity and impropriety in venues ranging from Australia House to the Queen's bathroom, the editor, like the Australian Customs before him, banned the strip from *Private Eye*. Was it, Colin Welch asked, one frustrated and flawed puritan taking it out on another? The character, however, lived on in book, and film and song.

Humphries and Garland produced a third book of Bazza's adventures, this time largely in Australia, the 'new Australia' of the 1970s in which all the men obediently sported Dennis Lillee moustaches. Bazza's widowed mother — between her scream therapy sessions, jazz ballet classes and Indonesian lessons — marries an androgynous Bondi hairdresser in the Botanical Gardens, while his brother Kev the Rev (or Kevin Menzies Nelson Eddy McKenzie) now sports a Gays for Christ T-shirt and runs a homosexual church, St John the *Divine*, with sauna and disco in the crypt. Kev's wife, Cherylene, explains that Kev is 'a metaphor for the intellectual ferment' that has transformed Australia while Bazza has been in England.

In the two movies — *The Adventures of Barry McKenzie* (1972) and *Barry McKenzie Holds His Own* (1974), both directed and co-written by Bruce Beresford — Bazza was played by the broad-jawed Australian singer, Barry Crocker, and Humphries himself played a number of roles: a still dowdy Edna Everage, the racketeering folk-singer Hoot ('If we can't make money out of this colonial hick, I'll quit this racket . . . er, I mean idiom'), and the psychiatrist, Dr Meyer de Lamphrey (a Humphries look-alike who is reduced to an alcoholic wreck by Bazza's case). The first movie, which followed the strip closely, had a brilliant cast, with Spike Milligan as a crazy, rapacious Earl's Court landlord; Peter Cook as a poisonous BBC television producer; Dick Bentley as a kinky Vice Squad detective; Dennis Price as a perverse public school old boy who, in shorts, cap and a Melbourne Grammar tie, hands Bazza a cane pleading, 'Thrash me, sir. Do with me what you will'; Avice Landon as his grasping wife; Julie Covington as an on-the-make folk-singer who belts out Bazza's beach song, 'The One-eyed Trouser Snake'; and Joan Bakewell who plays herself and addresses Bazza in a television interview: 'Most of us think of Australia as a tough, uncompromising land stricken by drought and flood, and inhabited by kangaroos and tough, insensitive, foul-mouthed beer-swilling boors. Yet . . .'

The Australian critics were primly scornful. Padraic
McGuinness found only 'vulgar rubbish', Ron Saw, 'a clumsy
vulgarity', Max Harris the 'Worst Australian Film Ever
Made' and Dennis Altman, 'perhaps the most vicious
anti-homosexual film of all time'. The English critics were
more generous, finding that the cameo roles and the scenes
of the Young Conservatives' jam-bang, of the folk cellar and
the BBC programme about the Australian *avant-garde* artists
made up for the blemishes. Christopher Hudson found it 'a
solid laugh from start to finish ... a humdinger not to be
missed'. David Robinson liked the film's 'high spirits', John
Coleman admired Crocker as 'the innocent abroad' and
George Melly the 'irresistible dainty certainty' with which
Humphries as Mrs Everage alternately sucked up to and then
patronized 'the poor little English people'. Only Nigel
Andrews found the whole thing 'unfunny and atrociously
directed'. In any case the film broke records. In both
Australia and England it was the most popular and profitable
Australian film yet made.

Humphries ridiculed the sour-grape critics who 'played
the fitful laser beams of their guttering intellects' so
mercilessly on 'the McKenzie world of featherweight fantasy'. But the allegation that he was anti-homosexual stuck
him as the most risible:

> Of course only a real dunce believes that the bigotries of a
> fictitious character are shared by his inventor, but the
> interesting question is, does Bazza *really* hate poofs any
> more than he hates Poms? I would have thought that they
> scared him stiff, or, rather, flaccid, and I am in a good
> position to vouch for this. Perverse travesties of coitus
> scare him silly. More than once I have described him as a
> *latent heterosexual*, and his every poignant blunder rein-
> forces the notion. Terrified out of his wits by poofdahs, he
> is equally wary of nymphos. *Everyone* is a sexual threat to
> Barry McKenzie and his fear is expressed by his absti-
> nence.

The second film was also a popular success but not on the same scale. Barely based on the *Private Eye* strip at all, it exploited Humphries' interest in gothic tales and Dracula stories: Count Plasma of Transylvania (played by Donald Pleasence), convinced that Edna is the Queen in disguise, has her kidnapped by his agents, Hugo Cretin (Louis Negin) and Modeste Imbecile (Paul Humpoletz). Rescued by Bazza's mates, Edna returns to Sydney in triumph to be created a Dame by Prime Minister Whitlam (played by himself in a probably unprecedented case of a serving Prime Minister acting himself in a Dadaist farce). Parts were also found for Tommy Trinder (the ghost of Bazza's ancestor), John Le Mesurier (a would-be Pommie migrant), Ed Devereaux (Sir Les Patterson's predecessor as Australia's Cultural Attaché in London) and Clive James (a left-wing film critic and toss-pot).

A typical scene is where Bazza, disguised in Arab robes, is entering England illegally with a van of Indians (including a snake-charmer with a cobra), and catches the attention of a police sergeant (Frank Windsor) and a police constable (Deryck Guyler):

[Van with Indians and BARRY enters an English village and stops. DRIVER opens the back.]

DRIVER: Comfort stop.
               [With tremendous speed all the Indians alight.]
BARRY: Must be the flamin' curry.
               [The Indians rush through a door. There is a sign. NATIONAL ASSISTANCE BOARD — UNEMPLOYMENT BENEFITS.]
SERGEANT: This your vehicle, sir?
BARRY: [Looking in the direction the Indians went] Ah...er...That's right, sport.
SERGEANT: [Recognizing his accent] Australian are you, sir? That yer national costume? Born in this country, sir?

[CONSTABLE laughs appreciatively.]

BARRY: Born in this . . . you've got to be kidding.

SERGEANT: [Annoyed] Indeed, sir? Passport, please,
                sir. [Barry gives it to the SERGEANT who
                hands it to his subordinate. SERGEANT
                looks around the van.]

SERGEANT: That your basket, sir?

BARRY: Yeah . . . it's, er, me dirty washing.
                [The SERGEANT puts his hand in the
                basket, then withdraws it quickly with
                the cobra wrapped around his wrist. He
                screams and forces it loose.]

SERGEANT: [Furious] Do you have a licence for this
                serpent, sir?

CONSTABLE: [Who has been checking the passport]
                Excuse me, sir, look at this. No entry
                stamp! This man is an illegal immigrant.

SERGEANT: [Pleased with himself – sarcastic] Well,
                well, welcome to England – cobber. We'd
                better find you a bit of accommodation.
                (Moving BARRY towards the police car.)
                And bring your cobra, cobber.

CONSTABLE: [Appreciating the joke, fawning] Oh very
                good, sir.

SERGEANT: I like your clobber, cobber.

CONSTABLE: Oh, wonderful, sir.

SERGEANT: I'm really chuffed to meet you, cobber. I
                tried to migrate to your bleeding country
                a couple of years ago and got knocked
                back, didn't I?

BARRY: I'm not surprised, mate. They're making
                it tough these days. You gotta be able to
                read and write before you can be a
                shit-house attendant.
                [SERGEANT bangs the door of the police
                van shut.]

[INTERIOR. OLD STONE BRIXTON PRISON CELL. BARRY is inside clutching the bars.]

POLICEMAN'S VOICE: You're going to be the guest of Mother England for some time, cobber. [Policemen laugh.]

BARRY: Lemme outa here! There wouldn't be no flamin' Mother England if it wasn't for Australia. Our fighting men come over here just when you Poms are ready to throw in the towel. Musso and his slimy yellow Nips would've flattened this dump if it wasn't for my uncles and their superlative fighting spirit. The game was nearly up for youse Poms, no risk. If it hadn't been for Australia, Musso and them slant-eyed pricks would've strung up every white kiddy by the pills and gone chock-a-block with all the nurses and bus conductresses. LEMME OUT YOU UNGRATEFUL POMMY BASTARDS!!!

The films made Humphries and his world more widely known than the strip alone could ever have done. After the movies he ceased to be a cult figure and the period of his enormous popularity began. If Bazza himself was by then a played-out, if well remembered, joke, Dame Edna was just beginning her career as a megastar.

Bazza did make a brief comeback in 1988 – the year of Australia's bicentenary – when Humphries and Nicholas Garland republished their three books in one volume ('not so much a legendary strip, more a resonant social history *per se*', proclaimed a Humphriesian blurb on the cover) with some new material for new readers. Bazza, still in London but now blind after a lifetime's self-abuse, is rescued from the gutter by Dr de Lamphrey and taken to a Chinese doctor who restores his sight by surgery on 'Mrs Palm and her five

daughters' (his right hand). Sir Les Patterson, who banned
Bazza in the old days, wrote a defiantly unrepentant preface
to this 'disgusting ... anachronistic ... travesty of an
Australia that never existed'.

11

A Gallery of Pseuds

A philosopher, when presenting his friend Barry Humphries with a copy of his most recent and ambitious book on the nature of the mind, remarked: 'It is my bid to be a footnote in the history of philosophy,' to which Humphries replied: 'what you must avoid is being a misprint in the history of philosophy.'

For his part Humphries has created a whole gallery of human misprints or pseuds and, himself a corrosive intellectual, has always enjoyed lampooning their pretentiousness. His first youthful Dadaist art exhibitions of 1952 and 1953 were parodies of more earnest post-Impressionist exhibitions and of their patrons who were meant to be shocked by his spoofing of Cézanne ('Yes! We Have No Cézannas!' was one offering), of Picasso ('Picassorole') and other fashionable heroes ('James Juice', 'Christopher Fried'). His 1953 university revue *Call Me Madman!* also mocked the easy humanitarian pieties of his student audience. For the last night of *Rock 'n' Reel Revue* in 1958, he created a stale theatre critic, Ern Deadpen, who summoned the actors on stage one by one to award marks to them all, except Humphries and O'Shaughnessy, whose existence he queried, and then proceeded, peering through opera glasses, to criticize the performance of the audience. In 1959 one of his first television shows ridiculed a blue-stocking pundit who had just returned from Communist China with a stock of travellers' tales.

But in the following years, 'while Beatlemania held sway and flower children, unshod, shuffled Sharon Tate-ward', Humphries paraded a whole series of New Age beatniks, hippies, folk-singers, film-makers, journalists, clerics and free-thinkers, all quite unlike their hobbledehoy cousins in the Humphriesian family. All are vain, tense and self-obsessed. Some, but not all, are hustlers. Most are sad figures, even when successes, and some have the obvious autobiographical touches common in Humphries' sketches.

Some have already been noted: the unnamed journalist, denouncing expatriates; Morrie Tate, the duffel-coated guitarist; Big Sonia, the microskirted folk-singer; Hoot, the hustler, and Martin Agrippa, the revolutionary film-maker and *auteur*. Others in the gallery include Craig Steppenwolf, the radical schoolteacher, co-written with Ross Fitzgerald. ('You know, it wasn't long ago in this very country of Australia, that illiteracy was a dirty word. Incredible, isn't it? In the bad old days of élitist right-wing education, universities actually barred students from their faculties merely because they were unable to read, write or count and remember? Thank Christ for Labor!') and Brett Grantworthy, a Hoot turned broker of expanding government subsidies for artistic charlatans, who urges (on the telephone) one client to apply for a grant under the Aboriginal programme:

Hold it, Sasha; look mate, whatever they do, they'll never cut back on bread for the boongs. Any Aboriginal blood in your family? How are they going to prove your grandmother was born in Russia? Couldn't she have migrated there from Alice Springs? The funding committee is but desperate. They'll believe anything. No, no birth certificate. No blood tests. Look, they got five hundred thousand to unload! They only need one applicant claiming he's a quarter-caste who isn't wearing yellow thongs and drinking metho, and they'll give him the lot.

By the way, Sasha. You're an old mate. But when we

swing it, don't forget my thirty per cent commission. Let's face it, I'd black up, change me name to Jacko and apply myself but I can't afford to cop another grant this financial year. Talk to you later!

A refrain in this conversation is: 'The old Moratorium spirit still holds.'

One of the greatest of Humphries' intellectuals is Neil Singleton, who first trod the stage in Australia in 1965 and London in 1969. With his long hair, fringe of beard without moustache, his pipe, his wine and his elastic-sided boots, audiences immediately recognized this denizen of Sydney's Paddington or London's NW1. 'I had no idea,' Humphries wrote, 'how many real Neil Singletons would emerge from the woodwork. Until the mid-sixties, Neil's class of puritan, querulous, turtle-necked, elbow-patched, pipe-sucking, wife-cheating, wine-buffing, abstract-art-digging highbrow had been amongst my most enthusiastic fans, eager for a chuckle at the middle-class effusions of Edna, Sandy and the other Australians they never met at their own parties. Deep chagrin greeted this impersonation; it was only after the birth of Neil Singleton that the arty periodicals really got stuck into me.'

He made his début in a butcher's apron carrying a teak cheese platter. He was expecting friends for drinks. The despairing trumpet of Miles Davis is heard. He greeted his guests: 'Welcome to our private hell'; 'I hope you've brought that superb woman of yours with the Lawrentian armpits'; 'If I was queer I could go for you in a big way', and described his new house: a primitive painting by an old tram-driver above the 'book storage unit'; a brick wall which said, 'I am brick, take it or leave it', a Brett Whitely litho, a Nolan, a Dickerson near the bog: and a fibre-glass chair that took some getting used to but had a superbly organic shape. In the neighbourhood was a *kabuki* restaurant – 'terrifically pleasant if you don't mind eating southern Jap . . . We usually go there when my slut can't be bothered cooking.' He had three children, Sibion (who 'picks up a load of suburban crap at school and loads it on to us'), Adam (three and a half years, to whom Neil just gave a lesson in sex education), and Natasha. His wife Karen, a chain-smoker and karate student, flirted with a show-business homosexual before retreating to bed; the principal guest did not come; the other guests left early; and Neil, a lonely figure, shouted 'Bloody poofdah' to the pitiful, empty room. It was the first time the free-thinking intellectual had appeared on the Australian stage. There was an excited shock of recognition and Neil Singleton entered Australian folklore along with Edna, Sandy and Bazza.

By 1974 Neil Singleton had become a heavy-drinking cultural pundit with a Zapata moustache and a regular television programme on which he discussed his forthcoming book about life in a commune. 'The Bludgermindee Experience' (a 'free-wheeling, socio-aesthetic non-linear hyper-responsive work of involved and simplistic neo-fiction'). His own home, or 'urban ecosphere', was a suburban corollary to Bludgermindee. After his programme he visited his girlfriend's flat, removed his sunglasses to reveal a black eye, dabbed his nose with a blood-stained handkerchief, and announced that he had finally left his wife (although even this was a lie). When he furtively rang his wife ('You nearly blinded me with that Marea Gazzard ashtray') to explain that he had to get away for a few days to *start* writing his book on Bludgermindee, he discovered under a cushion, first the tobacco-packet of his girlfriend's other boyfriend, and then her vibrator. As the curtain fell he gazed blankly at the 'sex aid' while over the phone his wife irately called 'Neil! Neil!'

Trendy men of God have increasingly taken their places in the Humphriesian gallery of pseuds, such as Bazza McKenzie's brother Kev the Rev (in Paris for a theological conference on 'Christ and the Orgasm') or the Rev Nunn, the homosexual rector of the Church of Christ the Motorist with a drive-in Sunday Service and a car-wash during Communion:

> Dearly beloved brethren. I'm the Reverend Roger A. Nunn. Hello to you. And that means hello to you. And hello to you. And a big hello to you, too ... The Divine Revelation which shot me into the ratings came at a very human moment in my life, one morning on the seventeenth of February nineteen hundred and seventy-five. I was endeavouring to park my consecrated Cortina as close as divinely possible to the shopping mall ... Suddenly I knew the answer to the empty pew. And soon you will, too. And you. And even you.
>
> Inadequate parking facilities!
>
> And so was born the Australian Church of Christ the Motorist ...
>
> You would have thought that the establishment of this Kentucky-style liturgical lubratorium would have been enough for one man to accomplish in a lifetime. But my heart was troubled. And so, after one particularly hard and greasy day of my forecourt ministry, I came home and I took my little wife in my arms and I said, 'Graham'. I said 'Graham, this lie we have been living has gone on long enough. We're coming out, thou and I. Who cares what your workmates think? Sooner or later you're bound to win acceptance from your fellow Qantas stewards.'
>
> Finally, my new book and its theories may not change your life but they will certainly touch it. Don't miss 'Sexual Intercourse with Koala Bears – Aberration or Alternative Life-style?'
>
> May the force be with you.

In the 1970s the intellectual caste gradually ceased to be the object of Humphries' scorn and (with the exception of the film-maker Phil Philby) dropped out of his shows. Les Patterson and, increasingly, Edna Everage then took over as the vehicles for intellectual pretentiousness and fraudulence: as Dame Edna once admitted, she had always nursed a desire to play Mother Courage . . .

12

Bizarre: Mad Dr Humphries, Dandiacal Collector and Raving Ratbag

In a recorded (but never staged) sketch Humphries set out to demonstrate that a ratbag has, as it were, more than kangaroos in his top paddock. In soft American accents against syrupy music and gusts of scornful laughter, he asked 'What is a ratbag?' and answered:

A ratbag likes indoor golf, train-spotting, scotch and tonic, Australian postage stamps and Bruckner's Romantic Symphony. He likes phoning up on talk-back programmes, writing letters to editors, participating in Walk-athons, amateur hypnosis, folk music and bee-keeping. He hates pillows, central heating, champagne, James Bond movies, other ratbags and black jelly beans. His wife makes her own bread, rolls her own cigarettes, gets photographed at student demonstrations and attends a hypno-therapist to give up smoking.

Ratbags believe in the Divine Right of Kings, the Flat Earth Society, flying saucers, and the Book of Revelations. They have their ancestries traced, their faces lifted and eat Chinese food with chopsticks *when they're at home* and no one is watching.

When the garbage man says Merry Christmas and holds out his hand, a ratbag shakes it.

If you're a vegetarian, a Jehovah's Witness birdwatcher with five-coloured Biros in your breast pocket and you belong to a sky-diving club, you are a potential ratbag.

If you are a hippy over nineteen who thinks Shakespeare was a woman, Hitler was Jewish and if Beethoven were alive today he would be writing TV jingles, you are a transitional ratbag.

But if you read *The Great Gatsby* once a year, if you can whistle the Brahms Hungarian Dances, don't have a television set, grow your own marijuana and have just ghost-written the autobiography of a surf-rider, you are a terminal or raving ratbag.

After more of the same he concludes: 'And friends, this story is true ... I AM THAT RATBAG.'

But he omitted from the thesaurus several of his own favourite ratbag masks. One is the Mad Scientist (or some variation of it), usually fiendish but sometimes benign, often bombastic but sometimes good-humoured. In his youth Humphries played a fiendish Mad Scientist in an amateur surrealist film, *Le Bain Vorace*, in which in a paroxysm of evil laughter he poured acid into a bath; and a variation of the role in a student revue when as Commissioner for the Demolition of Historic Buildings ('Wheelem the Wrecker'), he outlined his master plan to abandon atomic tests in the desert and to stage them in metropolitan areas. In 1959 he reappeared as the keeper of the Peckham madhouse in *The Demon Barber*, in 1962 as the Australian Minister for National Identity in his first one-man show, and in 1965 (in his second) as the Public Relations guru, Dodd, masterminding various political parties and their leaders. He was also the author, in the printed programmes of the three one-man shows of the 1960s, of the 'Notes and Queries' about Smiler the Leper, the most famous Australian expatriate, now residing variously in Munich, Lisbon and Taxco (Mexico), whose reeking satchel carried such Austral souvenirs as a fuchsia-coloured Melbourne tram ticket exhibiting an advertisement for Stamina trousers, and newspaper clippings by the distinguished Australian critics N.V. O'Brine and J. Ellis.

In the Barry McKenzie *Private Eye* strip he was Dr Meyer de Lamphrey, the psychiatrist who treated Bazza: although he persisted with his probing questions ('What exactly is your relationship with your mother?' 'I'm her son.' 'What about your sex life? Is it healthy?' 'Stone the crows! It ought to be. I haven't had a chance to catch anything yet.') in the end McKenzie reduces him to an alcoholic breakdown – a version of the reversal of the roles of Tid and his psychiatrist which had failed to amuse the veterans' club some years before. There is also an occasional touch of the Mad Scientist in other Humphries characters, including Edna in her cruel frenzies. Over the years he has recurred in Humphries' publicity pictures, where, sometimes monocled but usually revealing a single, angry, Vathek-like eye, he glares at his readers. The Mad Scientist is a role, Humphries says, that comes easily to him.

Mad Dr Humphries also appears as a dandiacal collector of bizarrerie, not only, as he claims, of books for their binding (platypus, ape or human skin ...) of pictures (for their frames), or kitsch (for its own sake) but also of peripheral, literary and artistic curiosities: minor gothic novelists, obscure decadent romancers, unread *fin-de-siècle* poets. He is an editor and anthologist. One collection of the 1960s is *The Barry Humphries Book of Innocent Austral Verse*. Influenced by the English anthology, *The Stuffed Owl*, it is a sentimental compilation of disarming doggerel, mainly by bad poets but also by some good ones, whose affectionate tone is caught by the cover picture of a wide-eyed Humphries surrounded by Australian flora and fauna, painted by the late James Fardoulys, a Greek-born impresario, café-proprietor, taxi-driver and primitive artist. The poems are divided into Songs of Innocence, Songs of Experience, and Songs of People and Places. This First World War stanza from 'It's a Long Way from Dear Australia', a song of Experience by the irrepressible Mrs G.R. Coxhead gives the tone:

> We are leaving home and kindred, sweethearts, mothers, wives;
> For the Motherland is calling – we don't grudge our lives.
> We would rid the world of tyrants, purify the air
> By the downfall of the Germans; wait till we get there!

Humphries launched the book triumphantly at his old school, Melbourne Grammar and it became the basis of his, or Dame Edna's, 1973 recital at the Poetry International Festival in London.

A later anthology, *Barry Humphries' Treasury of Australian Kitsch*, is a collection of Aboriginal Toby jugs, bronzed koala ash-trays, Opera House bottle openers ... It is 'the first cultural encephalograph', Mad Dr Humphries declared in the preface, 'of the Australoid race' whose art is still uncontaminated by the practices of the 'prancing catamites and predatory mamelukes' of the trans-hemispheric art world. Dr Humphries had the satisfaction of knowing that his researches were not without influence: his collection included an expectorating toad fountain in Sydney's Botanical Gardens; soon after the publication of his *Treasury*, the Trustees removed the fountain.

But the most notorious of Mad Dr Humphries' collections was his first book *Bizarre* (1965), a compilation of lugubrious purple (or mauve) passages about flagellation, masochism, lesbianism, necrophilia and other perverse inclinations by such writers as J.K. Huysmans, Octave Mirbeau, Arthur Machen, Marcel Schwob, Alfred Jarry. It also included pictures of the now doomed race of side-show freaks: mongols, three-legged men, dog-faced women, and satirical cartoons by Siné and Bovarini, as well as some *jeux d'esprit* such as Barbara Blackman's epigrams about lips of various varieties or some poems by Mrs G.R. Coxhead, the very bad Australian poet and one of Humphries' favourites (who also appeared in his *Innocent Austral Verse*). His editorial, marginal notes on the contributors and their work display his detailed knowledge of obscure writers rarely noted in the standard reference books. These three examples catch the flavour:

Count Fanny's Nuptials, Being the Story of a Courtship, by Simon Arrow, was printed for private circulation, and published by G.G. Hope Johnstone in 1907. The influence of Aubrey Beardsley's superb novel *Under the Hill* is clearly evident in the book, and has led some to suppose that 'Simon Arrow' was a pseudonym for the youthful Ronald Firbank. However, in an extremely limited field, the work has a flavour of its own resembling somewhat a lithograph of Conder set to music by Cole Porter. A strong clue to the identity of 'Simon Arrow', is, moreover, afforded by an inscription in the editor's copy of this rare volume. It reads: 'With the author's Compliments – Love is my Theme! – G. Hope Johnstone.

Alfred Jarry (1873–1907), French symbolist poet and dramatist. His *Ubu Roi* was described by Arthur Symons as 'the first symbolist farce'. The characters were dressed as masked marionettes and the action was accompanied offstage by the music of fairies. Oscar Wilde wrote of Jarry in a letter to Reginald Turner, 'He is a most extraordinary young man, very corrupt, and his writings have sometimes the obscenity of Rabelais, sometimes the wit of Molière and always something curious of his own. He made his début by producing a play called *Ubu Roi*...the point of the play was that everybody said 'Merde' to each other, all through the five acts, apparently for no reason ... In person he is most attractive. He looks like a very nice renter.'

John Gawsworth (1912-) King of Redonda and serious bibliographer. His *Collected Poems* are regrettably out of print since several thousand copies were drowned in a damp cellar in 1948. Some five pages of his books are listed in the British Museum catalogue, and he had the distinction of being the youngest Fellow of the Royal Society of Literature, winning its Medal at the age of twenty-seven.

The book provoked strong reactions: In England W.H. Smith, the leading chain of book stores, refused to sell it — one of the last acts of censorship in Swinging England — and Philip Toynbee in his weekly review for the *Observer* found it a 'bestially vulgar compilation'. In Australia Craig McGregor called it a 'masturbator's handbook' (although Max Harris deemed it 'a personal act of purification'), but it was not declared 'a prohibited import' and the only official action taken against it was the decision of the Melbourne municipality of Moorabbin to withdraw the book from its library. 'You are not entitled to take liquor above a certain strength', the Mayor said, 'and the same applies to literature.' A delighted Humphries wrote to the Mayor:

Dear Sir,
First of all may I say how delighted I am to see the name of Moorabbin creeping into the international news. It is not before time since too few people at home and abroad associate the name of your delightful suburb with cultural matters. I meditate upon a day not too far off when Moorabbin will be the home of an international festival of arts. I know sir, that the affairs of Moorabbin must keep you extremely busy, leaving you little time for idle reading. In view of this, would you do me the honour of accepting a complimentary autographed copy of my

humble work *Bizarre* to study at your leisure so that the
good folk of Moorabbin are not deprived too long of the
pleasure of reading it. I shall be delighted to insert book
markers at the best bits.

Your obt. serv.

Barry Humphries

A few weeks later the book was returned to the Moorabbin
Library shelves (marked 'Suitable for Adults'). But Hum-
phries was unrelenting and published this poem about
Moorabbin as seen by one of its native sons, a lorry-driver:

> The traffic eased up past Saint Kilda.
> Hampton and Elsternwick were clear.
> Signs of the speculative builder
> Warned him Moorabbin must be near.
>
> Moorabbin flashed by one more time,
> Brick veneer and weatherboard.
> How he recalled hot days in wartime,
> Off to the beach in the family Ford.
>
> Moorabbin's progress had surely tamed her.
> God, how the place had gone ahead.
> He set to wondering how they named her —
> A homestead, a creek, or a black long dead?
>
> The chief librarian ate his pastie
> And set a match to his lunchtime briar,
> 'Good books, Mrs Dunn, need not be nasty',
> He said, as he stamped her Georgette Heyer.
>
> But the driver crouched in his lonely cabin
> Flicked his transistor on to jazz,
> 'Who would have reckoned old Moorabbin
> Would have come on the way she has.'

Part of the problem with the book was the tone, or as one critic put it, 'the revolting phraseology' of Dr Humphries' preface:

> A delight in folly and a profound pleasure in the presence of the marvellous and the gruesome is to be found in all people and cultures, and this faculty has not had occasion to atrophy in the present century.
>
> A taste for the perverse in art and literature has been nicely ministered to by the 'Decadents' of last century, later by the surrealists, and more recently by entire nations who have translated the hallucinations and speculations of poetry into real and cataclysmic terms.
>
> It is perhaps a relief, then, to retire from the lurid and all too imminent documentation of cruelty, grief, and death, which is the main burden of modern newspapers, films, and novels, and return to the dandiacal and bizarre conjectures of long whiles agone.
>
> Here we can contemplate in tranquillity the stunning variety of human nature, whether it be expressed poetically or teratologically. We have eschewed the bawdy in favour of the piquantly erotic; the purple passage has given way to the more titillating mauve; our literary monstrosities are credible, our freaks, caught by the camera, less so. The writings of the insane find an honoured place here, and give solace to those who find the modern utterances of 'sound minds' more disquieting.
>
> For the reader who finds detailed descriptions of circumcision rites among the Australians not to his taste, we would recommed a glance at the curious sonnets of Pietro Aretino, or our scholarly Bestiary of Science Fiction. We are not so anthologically purist that we cannot envisage between the covers of one book, Ben Jonson and the author of *Count Fanny's Nuptials*, nor so unpatriotic as to publish Marcel Schwob and Sacher-Masoch without including some gem from Matthew Phipps Shiel or

fragment from the rare author of *Poppies and Mandragora* and other neglected English geniuses, notably L.F. Wynne Ffoulkes.

This volume is addressed, frankly, to the jaded palate. To those who find a literary diet of steak and eggs curiously insufficient, and to whom the works of great painters are so much necessary but savourless roughage. Here we extol the lewd charms of the chorus-girl to those who would find virtue merely in the Prima Ballerina, and we would suggest, also, that the charnel house and the lunatic asylum have their place with cathedral and concert-hall in the cultural guide-books.

Then there are photographs and merry japes galore, for this is essentially a family book, and one which we confidently expect will stand on every shelf between *Pears Cyclopaedia* and *Mrs Beeton*.

The Times Literary Supplement in an editorial on the book condemned its 'cheaply facetious' captions (and its tendency to erode our capacity to be shocked by horrors). Toynbee, scorning Humphries' 'insufferable ... arch flippancy', parodied the 'vile whimsicality' of the preface with some verse of his own (which he implied was from the book) for a concentration camp concert:

> We are zee boys of Auschwitz camp
> And it's aus schwitz us preety sooon.

He was also 'entertained', he wrote with disgust, by the book's film sequence 'of the thalidomide mother trying to sit her limbless baby on a pot' – which was no more in the book than the Auschwitz song. The publisher, Paul Elek, corrected the Toynbee review and protested at W.H. Smith's censorship. But *The Times Literary Supplement* thought there was 'no conceivable reason why a bookseller should stock a book he does not wish to', although it thought he should at least agree to accept orders for it.

A measure of Humphries' dandiacal indifference to his critics was the prefatory boast of recovering and republishing fragments from such neglected English geniuses as L.F. Wynne Ffoulkes, when none of her writings was in fact included! It was the sound of her name that appealed. An Australian critic said that Dr Humphries may have created a monster that will live to haunt him, and indeed the book is always put in evidence whenever any puritanical critic wants to dismiss him as 'sick'. It is Humphries' least successful, least controlled or edited production. He later described it as 'deliberately tasteless, hybrid, morbid' although it found admirers on the continent who appreciated its *caractère insolite*. He continues to list it in his bibliography and it remains an episode of autobiography. But the future lay with the more accessible freaks that he put on stage.

13

'I Was Ill and Mad . . .'

Barry Humphries was to say of 1970 that it was a year when 'I was ill and mad'. It was indeed a year of collapse after many years of increasing pressure. His marriage to Rosalind would soon be dissolved ('I only wash his socks,' she proclaimed in headlines in 1968 in what was only an apparent good humour.) She established an art gallery in Melbourne, remarried and began a second family. He quarrelled and broke with his agent Cliff Hocking who had launched the one-man shows in 1962. The London season of *Just a Show* failed at the box office. His BBC series *The Barry Humphries Scandals* was savagely censored. To round off the decade the Australian Deputy Commissioner of Taxation issued a writ on him for unpaid income tax: the British censorship authorities, he said, at least let one finish the job; the Australian Treasury gives one cause to wonder whether the job is worth doing at all.

The BBC fiasco began in 1969 when, on the strength of his London show, the Department of Light Entertainment asked him to do a comedy of seven half-hour shows to be produced by Dennis Main Wilson (producer of the original *Goon Show*, the Hancock series and *Till Death Us Do Part*) and starring Dick Bentley, June Whitfield, William Rushton, Diana Dors and Rolf Harris. In collaboration with Jan Davidson, Humphries completed the scripts; they were approved; and filming began in October. But the BBC then

moved abruptly. Bruce Beresford's burlesque of the Underground Cinema, which had been a hit in the 1968–9 *Just a
Show*, was excised completely. ('The BBC,' Humphries
wrote, 'particularly objected to a sequence in which a
trouserless Nigerian ate a banana in reverse – it grew with
every mouthful. Presumably the whole film would have
been passed had the banana been black.') Then a scene was
banned in which a bald man sprinkles his head with hair
restorer, only to find that a tangle of hair unravels Rapunzel-
like from his armpit. ('Armpits, I was informed, ranked high
on the BBC's *index librorum prohibitorum'*.)

The next to go was the following chorus from a pantomine
about the bushranger Ned Kelly, in which Dick Bentley sings
the role of Old Mother Kelly and June Whitfield, who wants
to marry Ned, sings 'Waltzing Matilda':

MOTHER KELLY (singing): You are too innocent to feel a
Tender emotion for my Ned,
You're just an inexperienced sheilah,
And he's what we used to call – a Ted!

MATILDA:	I love the way he smiles.
MOTHER K:	Did you know that he's got piles?
TOGETHER:	But we love Ned Kelly all the same.
MATILDA:	I love his curly locks.
MOTHER K:	Yes, but have you smelt his socks?
TOGETHER:	But we love Ned Kelly all the same.
MATILDA:	The way he wears his clothes.
MOTHER K:	Have you seen him pick his nose?
TOGETHER:	But we know the boy is not to blame.
MATILDA:	I'd hang upon those great big lips and kiss him half to death.
MOTHER K:	Just wait until he's had a few and smell his rotten breath.
TOGETHER:	But though he's small and smashed and smelly He's our lovely Edward Kelly

> And we both love Ned Kelly all the
> same (exeunt dancing).

'I have yet to discover,' Humphries wrote, 'which BBC
mogul suffers from haemorrhoids or is a prey to the chronic
digital exploration of his nasal arcana,' but the entire chorus
was cut from the broadcast 'on the grounds of obscenity',
with the result that the mystified television audience heard
Dick Bentley sing, 'And he's what we used to call a Ted!'
followed by an abrupt cut to studio applause and the end of
the number.

Finally Mrs Everage's rousing tribute to British Spunk was
deleted. The song extolling British courage down the ages
was filmed in full colour with an elaborate décor of Union
Jacks. The George Mitchell Choir and a chorus of thirty,
supported by a full orchestra, together chanted: 'It was
Spunk! Spunk! Spunk! that pulled them through!' But,
Humphries lamented, 'the great nation to whom it paid
tribute' was unable to see it in 1969. (Philips issued it on a
gramophone record in 1972.)

The London failure – with the general public but not his
loyal followers – of *Just a Show* in 1969 was more than a
deep disappointment. It brought with it, as the Australian
press reported the London press, the most sustained and
bitter attack on Humphries that he had ever experienced.
The London critics of 1969, unlike the Australians of 1968
who had praised the show enthusiastically, saw it, in
Sheridan Morley's words, as 'a sustained hymn of hatred of
his native Australia' and, despite slides urging the audience
to *Emigrate Now!*, 'nothing I have ever seen about Australia
makes me feel less inclined to do so.'

Milton Shulman thought the show 'will appeal best to
Australia-phobes or Australian refugees'. Irving Wardle
thought Humphries sometimes comes 'pretty close' to the
'unlovable type of Commonwealth entertainer who special-
izes in flattering the metropolitan public by sneering at the

habits of his own country'. Peter Lewis detected 'a strong whiff of hatred' for Australia and Herbert Kretzner, 'hardly a vestige of affection'. The *Sun* found not even a 'hint of affection' and the *Daily Telegraph* 'plenty to hate in Australian life'. Humphries' Australia, the critics agreed, was a land of louts, drunks, philistines, bigots, bores and bums.

All of this was promptly taken up in Australia, where impugning Humphries' patriotism became a popular blood sport amongst publicists. One popular Sydney television talk-show host, Mike Walsh, declared that Humphries was 'our worst enemy' who was doing 'great damage to our image over there'. (Humphries asked: 'Who is Mike Walsh? He must be a singer because he has no sense of humour.') The New Zealand impresario, Harry M. Miller, made headlines with his declaration: 'That man Humphries is an idiot ... we have enough trouble convincing the world Australia is sophisticated. Yet we have this idiot ruining the country.' (Humphries replied that he would study Miller's Australian productions of *Hair* and *The Boys in the Band* to learn the art of patriotic playwriting.)

The present writer interviewed Barry Humphries at this time and raised the matter of the growing anti-Humphries campaign in some sections of the Australian media, despite his ever-increasing popularity with the public. He replied that he could not win:

Luckily I commute a bit back and forth. Last time I arrived at the airport two gentlemen of the press approached me almost simultaneously, and the first one asked a question that is quite commonly addressed to returning entertainers: 'Glad to have you back, Barry. Very nice to see you back in Australia. What are your plans? Are you going to stay in Australia for very long?' I was very interested in this because it is a trick question. I said I was going to do three television shows and then had to go back to London to do a series for the BBC. And he immediately said, 'Yes, we probably seem a little bit rough and ready to you now, a little dull and naïve compared to all your newfound friends in the West End of London.' I was a little bit chilled by this. Seconds later another microphone was thrust in my face and another voice said to me, 'We're very glad to see you, Barry. What are your plans?' I was very guarded at this point and I said, 'Oh well, I'm very glad to be back in Australia and as a matter of fact, though I've got this BBC series, I would very much like to be staying on and working here for some considerable time.' And he said, 'Yes, we heard that you weren't doing too well over there.'

Humphries was clearly hurt by the attacks and even mentioned one Englishman who, after seeing his show in London, had decided to emigrate because it proved that, whatever was said to the contrary, Australians are able to laugh at themselves. As to the critics who claimed that Humphries, like other expatriates, was satirizing a long-gone, backward country, unaware of the swinging, sophisticated new Australia, and that he was *living in the past* . . . Humphries replied that the accusation reveals the critics' deepest fear – the fear that the expatriates working in the metropolitan centres of the world are living *in the future* and that it is their critics in the world's provinces who are really living in the past.

Meanwhile the Australian taxation authorities, in pursuit of arrears, were examining the Humphries case and he was called in for a conference. 'They drew me along to their offices and I sat in this austere room with two people, one of whom I might say very closely resembled G.K. Chesterton's description: his hairline began with alacrity where his eyebrows reluctantly left off. One of these gentlemen – and I've nothing against Catholics – said, "We have quite a dossier on you, Mr Humphrey." He even got the name wrong and there on the desk was the biggest book of press clippings I've ever seen. So I said: "You're obviously very

interested in my work, Mr O'Halloran." That wasn't his
name really, something rather like it – a good Church of
England name. "You seem so interested in my work and – if
we can forget Income Tax for a minute – tonight is the last
night of my show. Would you like to come along?" He said,
"Oh no, that won't be necessary. Oh no, my son has been to
... er ... one of your ... er ... er ... shows and he has told
me quite a bit about it, all I will need for my purposes." '

Humphries settled his tax problem, but the experience of
reading in the press about the writ to be served on him
before he received it could not deepen his affection for the
Australian authorities. At this time his offer to go to
Vietnam to entertain the Australian troops was totally
ignored. (It did not receive a written reply until an
Australian friend, Professor D.M. Armstrong, took up the
matter of this gross discourtesy with the Prime Minister's
Department.)
    But whatever the disappointments, quarrels, harassments
or humiliations of this period, an underlying problem of
alcoholism continued to grow worse. But drunks box clever
(as he put it) and as long as he could get away with it, he
ignored the grim warnings of doctors and continued to wear
the mask of the drunk as dandy: Clive James' memoir of the
1960s presents this Humphries' ('Bruce Jennings') disguised
as a monocled, latter-day Count Robert de Montesquiou,
swaying balefully in the middle of a party until he falls to the
floor to sleep it off, waking gradually to begin muttering
Australian advertising slogans from his childhood, *Aeroplane
Jelly for Me, Sydney Flour is our Flour* ... in the spirit of Sandy
Agonistes.

Humphries later gave a less romantic account of this
period:

I remember sitting in a taxi with a Harrods bag on my lap

that had half a bottle of whisky in it and looking at the
queue of heroin addicts outside Boots the Chemist in
Piccadilly Circus with contempt.

They were addicts and I was something else. I was, if
you like, a genius out of luck. I was a sensitive person. I
just drank alcohol like all the best people, like Dylan
Thomas, like Scott Fitzgerald, like Malcolm Lowry, like
John Barrymore, like Tony Hancock. I belonged to the
aristocracy of self-destruction.

And who were they? The riff-raff, weren't they? They
stuck needles in themselves, they didn't vomit in public
lavatories like I did.

One of Humphries' 'hospital poems' of the 1960s, 'Food'
reflects this harsher mood:

> Delicious wimpy, steaming disc of health,
> Garnished with tumbled onions on a crisp halved bun;
> The peas were garden fresh, discreetly minted,
> The chips new-hewn deep fried in peanut oil;
> All these, and more, that modest menu hinted.
>
> Saliva started, then engulfed his teeth
> As he withdrew the lustrous fork and knife from their
>   hygienic and informative paper sheath;
> Almost too good to eat, that asymmetric yet exquisite
>   meal —
> So, tucking in, and glad he'd eaten little else that day
> His first assault dealt instant disarray to the neat dinner.
> He felt almost like a sinner, so to despoil those chips
> Cooked with such love in purest peanut oil, or like a
> Vandal, when but half-way to his lips
> Some fell, and littered the formica.
>
> Tomato sauce had now completely blurred
> The contours of the meal,

And a large turd of Colman's mustard threatened to
   violate
All that remained on his plate.
His munching grew reluctant;
Films of milky fat were fanning fast
Over the smashed surfaces of that repast.
Pinching a comma of gristle from his teeth
He quickly tidied up the loathsome plate
Having derived some meagre goodness from it
And rushing out before it was too late
Searched wildly round for some quiet place to vomit.

Humphries returned to Australia in 1970 ('ill and mad')
heading for the inevitable crisis – a condition only deepened
by the gloating of 'friends' – as he depicted them in a playlet
of the time, *Welcome Home Mate*. A 'Drunken Ex-Pat' is the
obvious Humphries figure, and Desmond (who might be 'a
disappointed actor' and 'possibly a long-displaced Irishman')
is the host at a party in an outer Melbourne suburb: One
guest promptly refers to the poor reviews of the Ex-Pat's last
show in London. ('What exactly was the trouble?') Another
adds truculently that 'people here are becoming a wake-up
to you . . . You've been ruined by cheap success'.

When the Ex-Pat shouts back, 'You are just a bloody flop
and so are the lot of you,' Desmond is triumphant: 'Frankly
we feel a bit sorry for you, sport. Just look at the way you've
been boozing since you got back.' As the Ex-Pat collapses on
the floor in front of his gloating companions, he mutters,
'You'd booze too if you kept running into malicious shits like
you. I'm sorry I ever came back to the bloody place.' But
Desmond (secretly withdrawing a cigarette from his pocket
to avoid an expensive round) has the last word: 'Sorry to
hear that, mate, really sorry. We all knew you'd have trouble
readjusting to the realities of the Australian life as we live it
here. You may be right. London probably is the only place
for specimens like you.'

One the verge of a final breakdown and heavily sedated, Humphries was arrested in June and charged (in Camberwell!) with being drunk and disorderly and related offences. ('You pathetic bastard', he was alleged to have said to the policeman arranging his bail. 'It must have been a very dull day. You didn't have any old ladies to lock up.') A few days later he was bashed, robbed and left lying in a gutter. A woman eyewitness, who saw two men attack him, drag him down a laneway and tear a watch from his wrist, called an ambulance:

> If you want to put your feet up
> Relax and just unbend,
> There's a peaceful Richmond gutter
> That I highly recommend.

He was still able to open a Balinese art exhibition in his wife's gallery the next day, and he also managed a light-hearted 'Ballad of Camberwell Jail' beginning 'There's a little Chinese restaurant to the north of Camberwell' which included the lines:

> With his face as white as death
> And Wolfe Schnapps on his breath
> He was escorted to a room without a view.

In the Camberwell court hearing, the magistrate decided, in the light of Humphries' medical condition, to adjourn the case for six months and then to let the charges be withdrawn if there were no further incidents.

By the end of the year the fate that had loomed over him for so many years – as it had over so many of his literary and artistic heroes, from Ronald Firbank to Scott Fitzgerald, from *fin de siècle* poets to post-war Dadaists – overtook him and he finally cracked up. 'It was a desperate time,' he said

later, being enslaved by a chemical. 'You have to be almost
right at the end and unemployable before deciding whether
you pick up the gift of life or simply go down the tube.' In
the last days of 1970, and in, a friend said, 'an unspeakable
condition . . .in a high state of fragmentation, both economi-
cally and professionally,' with perhaps only weeks to live,
the man who for ten years, since the age of twenty-five, had
been taking an early morning drink, booked into Delmont, a
Melbourne private hospital specializing in alcoholism and
began the treatment which led him to become a cheerful
abstainer – and one of the greatest comedians of his age:

> Soon he'll forsake his catatonic trance,
> Shampoo'd and shaved, his belly back in trim,
> Easily scratched, but sober – there's a chance
> You might have stuck around to welcome him.

14

A New Outrageousness

If in the 1960s Barry Humphries confused interviewers with his often unkempt appearance, his lank hair reaching his shoulders, the soles out of flopping shoes, and a tendency to shout across the street in stern if patient headmasterly accents to some enraged, long-haired Ted: 'Son! Son! ... Haircut! Haircut!', in the 1970s it was an elegance or at least a smartness that impressed – his Eton crop (or as one reporter put it: hair Army sergeant short), his Savile Row suit (or his disguise, another reporter wrote, as the business-man he likes to think is struggling to get out), his Bond Street hats (usually a fedora), his Jermyn Street shirts. He became more publicly what he had always been privately: a dandy and aesthete, although one of regular hours: on one account, rising early, lemon juice at breakfast, hot shower, attending to business, light lunch, afternoon sleep at four, cold shower, early to the theatre, playing gramophone records after the show, a milk drink before sleep ...

He had donned, he said, a new and more irritating mask, bequeathing his old outrageousness, like his long hair, to the dull and boring who eagerly adopted it. 'I passed it gladly to them, having used it all up.'

This 'new Humphries', both funnier and darker, was not the simple result of his renunciation of alchohol, or ethyl alcohol as he sometimes calls it. Certainly the abstinent life brought its social difficulties. He has to avoid or frustrate the

Hospitality Bore at parties who insists that you have a *real* drink and will try to spike whatever you are drinking. He advises a cup of tea as a useful prop: the most determined Hospitality Bore seems reluctant to add vodka to *that*. Otherwise, 'No thanks, I'm already pissed,' may be effective, and 'I'm allergic, I'm afraid', often works in north London. But he did not become, he says, a tambourine-banging advocate of ginger ale and Jesus, although he has sometimes argued that schoolchildren should be taught more about the effects of alcohol and that producers of booze should be required, like other manufacturers of comestibles, to list on labels the chemical constituents of their products. Sobriety also became, in the words of his friend, Clyde Packer (his manager for part of the 1970s), 'a central part of his life'.

But artistically his freedom from alcohol removed if not an incubus at least a drag, as the new and more savage persona was released. It was not entirely new. It had been gradually emerging in the 1960s in the 'dandiacal rage' that John Wells described and in the blasts against fraudulence in *Just A Show* which English critics in 1969 mistook for a loathing of Australians. It was clear already in his prolific newspaper journalism in the months before his breakdown at the end of 1970. Sometimes he would write as a sort of Tory-anarchist diarist recording with gothic disgust the simian follies of the age: denouncing the government's policing of the literary grant which in desperation he had taken; tormenting an imaginary catamite or sex-changing servant; or flourishing an obscure or obsolete vocabulary: hircine, atrabilious, fescennine, lucifugous, nacreous, cachinnatory, ludibrious, paughty, gimp, algid, tabid. Sometimes he put new characters, all phonies, whom he was working up, through their first paces: the Rev. Neil Scriminger (an early Rev. Roger A. Nunn) who discerns a Christian message in Kenneth Tynan's nude masquerade *Oh, Calcutta!*: Ken Frankenstein (a precursor of Les Patterson), a profoundly philistine Minister for Culture; Ken Goniff (a model for Morrie O'Connor), a shonky art dealer who can always 'restore' a signature; and Damien Crawley (a friend of Neil Singleton and Craig Steppenwolf), a Vietnik embittered by the refusal of the fuzz to arrest him for his *Students' Guide to Shoplifting*.

Sometimes he was a literary critic who selected for review books which illustrated for him different aspects of the world's dishonesty. Only one review stood out for its enthusiastic acclaim – of Patrick White's *The Vivisector*, but this epic novel was about a satanic voyage and White, Humphries wrote, could depict Vulgarity in all its magnificence:

> Yet one turns to a new book by Patrick White fearfully, all the same. The events he chronicles are so strange but so compellingly, repulsively familiar. We discover his freaks within ourselves, his outlandishments [*sic*] illuminate and exorcise all that was painless and prosaic, asleep inside the pretty Sali Herman houses. The sexual encounters are so unbearably tremulous and personal one can never be an armchair voyeur, but an engulfed participant.
>
> And after each sabbatical of tenderness and lust, the Vivisector climbs or is driven back to his cell, his ramshackle Paddo attic, hunted back there to the seediness to assuage his vice, his inexorable Art.
>
> The book charts his satanic voyage.

The comic Humphries reasserted himself in the last words of the review: ' ... it is Patrick White's greatest book, unless you care to reread the others. Any questions?'

In the 1970s, as he resumed, and increased, his familiar breakneck pace, producing sketches, records, books, essays, films, there were several new departures in his life and art. He began supporting, for example, programmes for famine relief or wilderness conservation and he became a voluntary purchaser for the South Australian state Art Gallery ('an excellent provincial gallery'), acquiring for it in Prague, Paris, Brussels and London a collection of comparatively inexpensive drawings by 'great artists of the second rank' (Francis Picabia, George Grosz, Ernest Ludwig Kirchner, Aristide Maillol, Alphons Mucha, Fernand Knopf). He also made an extraordinary recording of Sandy Stone chanting the Lord's Prayer – a heart-rending performance as this limited, drawling, good man senses the wonder of God, seeks His forgiveness, forgives the rest of us, asks not to be led into temptation, and proclaims: 'Thine is the kingdom, the power and the glory for ever and ever', before falling exhausted into a coughing fit.

Above all the Splenetic Commentator, intimated in the 1960s, now found full voice – a critic whose Baudelairean spleen is quickly aroused by the contemplation of Australia, a country which obsesses him far more than is generally acknowledged. Even leaving aside all his Aussie stage characters, few people and fewer entertainers have had so much to say about Australian public affairs in countless interviews, articles, essays, speeches, odes and songs – and almost all his observations are censorious, if not didactic.

His rage is commonly (but not always) expressed with humour: 'The perennial question for Australians,' explains Dr Humphries, 'is, do we inhabit God's own country or the *anus mundi*? Therein lies so much of our identity crisis.' The Koala Triangle between Sydney, Melbourne and Auckland is,' he reports, 'a mysterious zone in the southern hemisphere where persons of talent disappear without trace'. In London, 'they used to ask me why so many talented Australians have to go overseas. But we *have* progressed. Thanks to Australian Council subsidies we are now exporting in large numbers people with *no* talent whatsoever. To be 'Australia-based' means, he says, to be 'a person of diminished aspiration who has been successfully bribed with grants and awards to resist the lure of expatriation'. His definition (or, to be precise, Les Patterson's) of a pan-handler is 'an

Australian playwright'. The Melbourne Cup, a sort of Australian Ascot, is 'one of the few social events in the world where public drunkenness by women is encouraged.'

Sometimes it is the melancholy seer who reflects on his countrymen: 'We are the next lot of Aborigines. There will be kindly, philanthropic Orientals worrying about our booze problems. Perhaps giving us huge sums of money to stay out of town, gathering us up from park benches, railway sidings and from under bridges, cleaning us up and hoping it will be all right next time ...' Sometimes it is the censor of complacent Australian clichés who speaks: 'Australia is one of the *worst* places in the world for children. There's not even a decent pantomime at Christmas. There is very little cultural recreation for children. I certainly didn't enjoy my childhood tremendously in Australia.' Sometimes there is undisguised rage:

> You have to see who are the people ruling our lives ... car salesmen, developers, disc jockeys, television hucksters, gourmet writers, mistresses of newspaper owners, gossip columnists, corrupt aldermen, ineffectual Premiers, talentless arts administrators, or self-seeking journalists. Then you must present them in an amusing and theatrical way to hold some kind of mirror, albeit fogged, or cracked, for the reluctant scrutiny of the public.

Philistine developers, pompous politicians and resentful hacks – always Australian – constantly enrage him. A proposal to erect a colossal shopping mall in his home town, Camberwell, provoked a thoroughly unamusing letter to the press: the charming suburban streets, he warned, will become traffic feeders for this monster, which will inevitably attract 'hoons, car thieves, druggies and yobbos'. He concluded: 'Something smells. Wake up, Camberwell.' A proposal to demolish the wonderful Romanesque Queen Victoria Building in Sydney provoked a bitter poem about 'the noose of progress':

> A casino, car park or urinal
> Would grace such a site.
> The end could be painless and final,
> The deed done by night.
> Reactionary ratbags won't budge us
> Nor sentiment sway;
> But how will posterity judge us
> Ten years from today?

A City Council proposal to demolish Brisbane's Bellevue Hotel with its gracious coral verandas and cool old-fashioned rooms provoked this: 'It seems Australia's ill-luck that these jabbering and onanistic chimps swing from every chain of office in the land, defecating on each sweet architectural remnant we possess.'

As for politicians, he has, almost from the beginning of his stage career, engaged in public debate with many of them, including the times when sycophantic journalists tried to protect them from critical publicity. At a time when the Australian politician (later Prime Minister) Robert Hawke, yielding to pressure from his own left wing unions, had ignored Lech Walesa's pleas for support, Humphries described Hawke as 'a statesman known to Polish trade unionists as "Hawke the Silent".' When one philistine Minister for the Arts ordered his State Gallery not to use Humphries' volunteered services as a fund-raiser on television, Humphries lampooned him on stage for years afterwards as an absurd, provincial boor and the foul-mouthed presiding officer of a corrupt administration. When a Senator denounced the Bazza movies as damaging Australia's image, Humphries called for the international networking of Parliamentary broadcasts 'to show the world what a race of dignified, eloquent sophisticates we really are'.

Some of his sharpest barbs are reserved for the 'Grub Street prigs, the claret-faced hacks, the discjockracy of Australia'. Most disc jockeys, he claimed, have the OBE: 'It's a prize for mediocrity.' This is how he described Australia's probing television interviewers:

> We are invited to participate in some 'in-depth' television scrutiny which, in Australia at least, means a few tongue-loosening Mickey Finns in the Hospitality Room, a revolving leather armchair, blazing third degree spotlights which would have blown the electricity budget of the Gestapo during a busy week, and two cameras, one trained on the interrogator's hispid occiput, and the other in merciless proximity to the victim's face to record every Max Factored tic, every tell-tale nictation and every embarrassed grimace. Meanwhile the microphone hovers like a carrion crow or voracious vulture ready to devour any morsel of shed dignity, chapped ego or drop of blood which the interrogator may succeed in extracting from his hapless (and usually unremunerated) prey.

In an apparently more resigned mood, he wrote an ode to Australia's media stars:

> It's so nice not to go to the theatre,
> It's so restful not opening a book.
> It's sheer ecstasy
> Just to eat, sleep and pee,
> Then switch on the set and just look . . .

Barry Humphries, in short, is one of the few free-thinkers willing to tell the Australian emperor and his court that they have very few clothes at all. But in the end Australia is simply the world on a small stage.

15

Legend

Early in 1971, the famous New Zealand-Australian show
business entrepreneur, Harry M. Miller – the man who had
managed the Australian tours of Sammy Davis Jr., Louis
Armstrong and the Rolling Stones, who had brought the
musical *Hair* and the homosexual drama *The Boys in the
Band* to Australia, and who in 1969 had called Barry
Humphries 'an idiot...ruining the country' – agreed to
manage Humphries' affairs and produce his next one-man
show. Miller later wrote that he regarded Humphries as 'in
need of stern management'. Humphries in turn enjoyed
baiting Miller. 'Barry was never the easiest of my clients to
manage,' Miller recalled.

At the time the two men reached agreement Miller was
amazed to receive a letter marked 'Confidential', signed by
'William McMahon, Prime Minister':

> My dear Mr Miller, I would like this communication to be
> treated as strictly confidential, and since I know you to be
> a man of integrity this goes without saying. Affairs of State
> have for some little time placed a considerable pressure on
> both my goodself and Sonia, and my long interest in the
> world of show business prompts me to 'put out a feeler', as
> it were, with regard to the position in your firm which
> has latterly become available. I would be grateful if you
> would keep me apprised of the situation as it develops in

this particular respect. I hope that you will not consider it impertinent of me to assume that you have a natural, indeed lively, interest in Her Majesty's New Year Honours List. With best wishes for your retirement . . .

Miller said he agonized over the letter. Why should the Prime Minister ask him for a job? What vacancy? Was the PM after Miller's job? Miller was buying a farm but he was only thirty-seven and had no intention of leaving show business. (He was in fact preparing the Australian production of *Jesus Christ Superstar*.) What did the PM mean about the Honours List? It was two days before a colleague told him that the letter was from Barry Humphries, who had somehow purloined a few authentic sheets of prime ministerial writing paper.

'During our time together,' Miller said good-humouredly, 'there was hardly a feature of my life that he did not send up on-stage and off.' The programme for the 1971 one-man show carried an identikit drawing of Miller over a statement attributed to him, in which Humphries ridiculed the high-seriousness with which Miller had sometimes presented his earlier productions (as well as his pioneering use of the word 'hopefully'):

> In the past my name has been associated with controversial, even 'permissive', theatre, so it will surprise Sydney audiences to see my name linked with, if Mr Humphries will forgive me, an 'establishment' entertainer. Not for him the *double entendre*, the satiric thrust or the bold iconoclasm of full frontal nudity. Not for him the harsh verities that are Vietnam, acid rock, drugs, homosexuality or the osmosis of the infrastructure of the whole Now Scene. Where you or I would seek enlightenment in the occasional writings of Artaud, John Cage or Buckminster Fuller, hopefully, profundity in the music of Erik Satie,

Led Zeppelin and Jimmi Pseud, and visual charisma in the art of John Lennon and Pro Hart, Humphries gives us a world of fantasy and escape. The conflicts and dichotomies of present-day Australian culture hopefully pass him by, as he leads us tenderly by the hand into his own cloud-cuckoo-land of cosy illusion. A lover of horses, women and money, he eschews the napalm-scared present, and offers us instead a nostalgic glimpse of your actual collective Dreamtime; a world which, had Verlaine been an Australian, would have hopefully (continued on page 96 . . .)

The show, *A Load of Old Stuffe*, intended as a retrospective or anthology programme re-presenting Edna, Sandy, Neil Singleton, Brian Graham and Martin Agrippa, opened in Sydney in April 1971 (with Iris Mason's 'eleven fingers depressing the keys of the pianoforte'). For Humphries it was back in the small halls again (the *Playbox* in Sydney and Melbourne) and a frugal production. (The credits listed 'Sets by St Vincent de Paul. Lighting by Electricity. Sound by Listening'.) The title was defensive but also misleading. While the duller critics referred to Humphries' 'exhausted' talent (since there were no new characters in the show) the better ones, such as Katherine Brisbane and H.G. Kippax, noted much that was new: a new 'savagery', a new 'vicious' and 'ruthless' satire, a new tragic dimension to the comedy.

It was certainly a new Edna – now a parody of high fashion and a predator of treacly sentimentality in black boots and glittering scarlet hot-pants split to the groin, she was becoming the Edna of legend, and the critics began to ransack the dictionaries for adjectives and descriptions: psychotic, hysteric, schizophrenic, dionysiac, crypto-fascist, Amazonian, anally obsessed, a tornado, a piranha, a vulture, a death-ray, a harpy, a hell-cat, a scrawny dervish, a hectoring Medusa, a blue-rinsed beast of Belsen, the Australian daughter of Torquemada. Increasingly a woman of name-dropping culture and radical views, she had left in her wake a series of broken lives – her hospitalized husband (at any sign of his recovery, she will get a second opinion); her institutionalized mother (in a high-security twilight home at Dunraven, St Peter's Close); a shop-lifting alcoholic daughter, and a homosexual son. She was also becoming one of the great comic-tragic inventions of the age.

Sandy Stone opened the second act again, reading, from a large bed, a series of letters to his wife Beryl who is visiting the Old Country. His world is now his Milo, his hottie, his birdie, his telly, his suppositories and a few neighbours: each letter repeated the same news, about watering the shrubs and 'giving your mother-in-law's tongue a drink', feeding the parrot 'a fresh slice of grannie [apple]' each day, sprinkling the Harpic toilet cleaner and applying his suppositories, both 'religiously' ... He kept her up-to-date about their neighbourhood and about the serials on television, and the two seemed equally real – or unreal. His friend, poor old Phil, who had a strained valve, was pottering around his brand-new home unit all day 'like a ghost' – but Phil was not the only one who seemed to be a ghost. Finally, as the glaring traffic rushed by, this Diary of a Nobody ends and Sandy dies, in his sleep. Almost his last words are: 'The Harpic is cleansing while I sleep.' There was hardly a dry eye in the house as the stoic simplicity of his limited life and its ending seemed to dramatize the vacuity of Edna's new world – the corrupt and exploitative show-biz world which Neil Singleton and Martin Agrippa secretly yearn to join. Humphries himself later wrote: 'I am pleased to say that this sketch always had a profoundly depressing effect upon those who saw it.'

The show toured Australia, but Humphries was not ready to take it to England again, and although Edna Everage continued her appearances on English television and radio and in the film *The Adventures of Barry McKenzie* (where she was still the old dowdy Edna), it was not until June 1973 — four years after the popular flop of *Just a Show* — that she returned to the London stage, at the ICA as one of the 'side-shows' of the annual Poetry International Festival organized by Charles Osborne. It was a decisive appearance. She arrived shrieking, laden with pearls, tottering on high heels, wearing a long vermilion skirt, carrying a volume called *The Cantos of Ezra Pound* (the public reading of which had been a high point of the serious side of the festival) and commenting: 'People think they can write about any part of the body these days.' Calling Charles Osborne 'John' and praising his plays, she proceeded to read selections from the 1968 anthology *The Barry Humphries Book of Innocent Austral Verse* (and from the 1972 recording of some of it). They included chauvinist Pommy-bashing doggerel, hymns of motherhood and songs of courtship:

> But oh! How we kissed on that very first date
> When the old needle hissed on a 78.

She concluded with her own celebration of Australians who had done 'terribly well' in England — Joan Sutherland, Rupert Murdoch, Skippy and Peter Finch:

> All your best dentists come
> from the Land of the Gum.

Dame Edna, in her 1989 autobiography, *My Gorgeous Life*, recalled the occasion:

> Mr Osborne invited me to do a poetry reading with two poets called Allen Ginsberg and W.H. Auden. I read some of my own works and some other lovely verses by Australian women, holding everyone spellbound; whilst the other two — wouldn't you know — gave the audience a really hard time, mumbling their own murky verses. Mr

Ginsberg's poems being more than a little on the uncalled-for side too! Mr Auden and I hit it off quite well backstage however, though his suit looked as though it had been slept in (by someone else) and the poor old thing wasn't exactly, as Norm would say, 'in showroom condition'. As Wystan and I nattered on about art and life, I gazed sadly at his creased old countenance. He didn't get a face like *that* from eating strawberries!

It was a success — Edna's first on the English stage. Julian Jebb wrote in *The Times* that 'since the retirement of Maria Callas, Humphries is the greatest star alive'. (This judgement, he added, was often met with ignorance or sarcastic laughter.) The general popularity of Edna's 'side-show' encouraged Humphries to start thinking about another one-man show in London.

But his next, *At Least you Can Say You've Seen It*, in 1974 was also an Australia-only show (although back in the big theatres, such as the Elizabethan in Sydney and the Comedy in Melbourne). Produced by Clyde Packer, who took over the management of Humphries' affairs, it introduced some new characters from the New Age: Brett Grantworthy, the arts grants broker; Neville Creamer, the closet homosexual; and Morrie O'Connor, the high-pressure, huckstering picture salesman in a sky-blue suit with flared trousers and a straw-coloured 'Beatles' hair-cut:

Now I know, ladies and gentlemen, that you or you can go to any fly-by-night back-street art dealer but you'll never get the value or the quality we can offer you here at Morrie O'Connor's. It's a moral they'll flog you some biffed-up grunter, some souped-up amateur crap heap with a dudded date and a smicked-up signature. These boys will get into your kick, get the fat off you and leave you with a dog on the wall. They'll stitch you up, stick it up you and take you for a dead-set dickhead.

Here at Austral Art, we can offer you an after-sales service second to none in the southern hemisphere. If you're after a grouse pose painting, we can sit you in front of a custom-built late nineteenth-century vintage Impressionist. Just state subject and colour preferred and our expert restoration service does the rest. We can arrange for you to meet the artists too – if they're alive or sober. If you're a dead set bona fide customer we can fix it for real artists to drop by regularly at your home and personally service your fleet of originals or even grace any social occasion you might happen to be throwing at the time.

Sandy Stone was revived from the dead to soldier on as a *revenant*: In 'Sandy and the Sandman' he browses through the Holy Trinity Opportunity shop, finding an old family album with snaps of gaitered First World War diggers 'with the sort of far-away look on their faces like they *knew* they was never coming back', and some later snaps of family pictures with everyone spruced up and trying not to look into the sun: 'They wouldn't have bothered, would they, if they'd known they was all going to end up around an opportunity shop with "15 cents" in chalk scribbled across the happiest days in their lives.'

For this show, Edna had become larger than life and one incredulous and contemptuous critic, reporting from Sydney for the *New Statesman*, turned to psychiatry to describe her: 'Psychotic ... hysteria ... schizophrenia'. She is already the sinister and insulting hostess of a *soirée maudite* and of an ever more frantic audience involvement. Now *Dame* Edna – having been honoured by Prime Minister Whitlam in the second Bazza McKenzie movie of 1974 for her services to Australia – she dressed from turban to high heels in a spoof of front-stall fashions and entered from the back stalls, handing boxes of 'chockies' to her guests as she asked their names, which, as in all later shows, immediately became ridiculous. (Sigrid: 'A lovely name. It just sounds like something you squirt into a room where people have been smoking.') She began the inexhaustible game of questioning people about their bedrooms and bathrooms, brought patrons on stage for delighted humiliation, bounced a giant polystyrene Jaffa chocolate ball over the singing audience's heads, hurled gladdies vindictively at the patrons and conducted the traditional finale with a gladdie between her legs as she shrieked, 'It's the bit on the tip that counts', or 'Hit the nearest Protestant'. When it was over the eyes of the gnomes around the auditorium lit up and flashed. One reviewer found it 'worse than a Billy Graham rally'. It was indeed something extraordinary. Never one to ignore a criticism altogether, Humphries wrote some years later that compared with the apotheostic splendours of gladdie-time, a Billy Graham rally or a Nuremberg rally – or a Melbourne football grand final – would appear boring.

It was during a return season in Melbourne of *At Least*, late in 1975, that he met the artist Diane Millstead. Attracted by an exhibition of her paintings – most of them 'blue, disquieting, fastidiously executed' and showing, despite influences of Magritte and Max Ernst, a 'shining originality' – he determined to track her down. He called at her studio after the show at about midnight, but finding that he had woken her from sleep, backed off apologetically and called the next day, sitting in an uncomfortable chair and discussing the Belgian symbolists and the Swiss painter of sea nymphs, Arnold Boeklin, whose works, like Humphries, she admired. She, who had expected him to be much older and not at all the 'tall, dark, handsome and interesting' aesthete he turned out to be, soon became his companion and later his wife.

Humphries was now almost ready to make another incursion into the West End. But first he needed to 'refine' the newest member of the Humphries family, his greatest curtain-raiser, the most famous of the products of Humphries' renunciation of alcohol.

16

Dr Sir Leslie Colin Patterson, KBE

As Mr Les Patterson (as he then was) staggered forward at the Apollo, Shaftesbury Avenue, in March 1976 and slurred for the first time at a London audience: 'Testing ... one, two, three, four ...fuck' and then disappeared back through the curtain, only to reappear with Scotch and cigarette ('Good evening, ladies and gentlemen ...can I have a little shush up the back?') and to urge patrons to give Dame Edna the clap she so richly deserved, the audience took this beer-bellied, good-humoured, revolting politician, now Australian cultural attaché, to their hearts. For ten minutes, Michael Billington reported, Les had them 'almost levitating out of their seats'. He was, Julian Jebb wrote, 'a comic creature of amazing force'.

At this time Les Patterson was still a barely known figure in Australia. An early and milder Les Patterson had first appeared, in January 1974, at a Sydney club and beer palace as its entertainments officer – a useful disguise when facing the sort of audience that had turned its back scornfully on Barry Humphries some twenty years before – whose job was simply to apologize for the absence of Sammy Davis Jr. and to introduce Dame Edna (into whom Humphries quickly changed during a musical break). Mr Les Patterson was not yet as foul-mouthed, as slobbering or as vilely dressed as later – he was taken to be a club official – and Humphries was not yet ready to present him to a wider Australian public. His appearance in a Hong Kong cabaret the following year as the

Australian cultural attaché passed unnoticed in Australia — although in Hong Kong, according to Humphries, some Chinese bouncers seized the drunken bum as he was staggering towards the microphone and tossed him out into the streets. The English merchant bankers and commodity brokers and the Australian accountants, however, recognized him as someone they knew in the diplomatic service and welcomed him warmly. It was his triumph in London in 1976 that brought his name to the attention of the Australian public at large — and engaged the disgust of both leftist and conservative prigs: one Labor hack found in Les Patterson (whom he had not yet seen) the final proof of the decline of Humphries' art and wit, and conservative *apparatchiks* deplored the way in which Les Patterson would damage Australia's image in England. But when the Australian public had the chance to see him as Dame Edna's foil and forward scout in 1978 in *Isn't it Pathetic at His Age?*, he immediately entered Australian folklore.

Sir Les (as he soon became) is the greatest of several of Humphries' ageing hobbledehoys, but he springs from a long line of kindred spirits. The first intimations were in two characters who emerged in the late 1950s. One, performed in the Assembly Hall, Melbourne, in 1959, was an unnamed derelict who frequented the municipal gardens of an evening singing (to the tune of 'White Sportscoat and Pink Carnation'):

In my white sand shoes and my Army greatcoat,
I'm all dressed up for the park.
In my white sand shoes and my Army greatcoat
My life begins . . . [*softly*] . . . after dark.

You'll find me [*suddenly vibrant*] behind the scoreboard.
You'll find me behind the pav.
And every Saturday arvo
My haunt [*now mumbling*] is the gentlemen's lav.

Immure me beneath the enclosure
[*speaking not singing*]
With an old jam jar and a sprig of gorse.
They'll say that I died of exposure.
[*grinning*] Indecent exposure of course.

In my white sand shoes and my Army greatcoat,
No longer I'll misbehave.
For in my white sand shoes and my snow-white
greatcoat...
... Great coat! [*his eyes aflame as he recalls better days*]
I'm all spruced up ...for the grave.

The sniggering or giggling audience would fall silent as he shuffled off to the strains of Chopin's 'Funeral March'. But the character was more an intimation of an aged and defeated Les Patterson than Les in his prime with all his relentless vitality.

The other early precursor, who appeared on record only, was Colin Cartwright, the embittered Melbourne businessman who cannot buy his family's love. ('The wife drops her eternity ring down the waste disposal unit in the sink. It wasn't insured, so guess who paid for that little issue ... I've usually got to buy my own Father's Day present,') but he was sober (at least in the sketch) and too apoplectic, bitter and humourless to be a Les Patterson.

Nineteen sixty-eight edged closer to the Patterson form when the drunken Rex Lear collapsed at his daughter's wedding breakfast after insulting the Italian head waiter. ('You were all brought up on the smell of an oil rag, a bit of garlic, and a few crucifixes anyway. You can't even paint your houses a decent colour.') Morrie O'Connor was another of the same bear-pit: the used-car salesman whose trousers barely concealed a huge foam-rubber phallus and who conducted a Magic Mile of Masterpieces offering ripper deals on new, used or superseded Sidney Nolans, some barely looked at. ('That's better than a kick in the Jackson Pollocks. See yez!') Lance Boyle, the corrupt, unprincipled, dissolute and irrepressible union boss was another, if slightly younger, member of the set.

In the 1970s they came together in Les Patterson, exuberant clown, revolting drunk and folk anti-hero, converting Humphries' disgust with alcoholic oafishness into, as Michael Billington wrote, a comic weapon. He took Rex Lear's vulgarity (without his malice) and Lance Boyle's lack of principle (without his rage) and combined them with Morrie O'Connor's groin and Barry McKenzie's flair for language (and booze), adding Les's own oafish, chauvinist good humour. Like all Humphries' major characters, he comes to us with a mythology – a full family life and *curriculum vitae*. Educated at Our Lady of Dolours in Sydney, he married Bambi Dolan, a former model – or more precisely a hand model ('that's her hand wiping the baby's arse') – and now a medical wreck (she has had more explorations than Les has made overseas missions) who sits watching TV all day and night in her pink chenille brunch coat and a pair of fluffy mules full of toast crumbs, 'sucking on a king-size St Moritz mentholated and sipping her way through a chilled cask' of cheap wine. They have two children, Craig and Karen, who, like most of the children of Humphries' principal characters (Edna's, Neil Singleton's, Lance Boyle's) are victims of their parents' heartlessness, although in Karen's case, 'thanks to her speech therapist, you don't notice anything unless she is nervous'. He is foul-mouthed (but will 'yield to none in his abhorrence of bad language' – in women); chauvinist (his ideal woman is three feet six inches high with a flat head – to rest his beer on); and alcoholic (hiding his vodka in the cistern, brandy in the fuse box, gin in his Masonic apron and flagons of wine under the house and whisky in the golf bag – under the cobwebs).

Inevitably drawn to the Catholic right-wing of the Labor

Party, he rose to be a Minister of the Crown (for, variously, Inland Drainage, Rodent Control or Shark Conservation) in the Whitlam Government in the 1970s and finally Australian Cultural Attaché to the Court of St James's. A famous public figure and friend of the powerful (although there is no truth in the rumour that he has been to a health farm and changed his name to Robert Hughes), his presence soon became necessary on all great national and international occasions.

Officially opening the Australian Research and Studies Establishment (ARSE) in Bloomsbury in 1982, Sir Les began by quoting his Prime Minister:

> Australia's international image needs a bit of spit and polish and you're just the man to put his mouth where Australia's money is. Let's face it, Les, our lanky leader went on to infer, London's chock-a-bloc with expat knockers making a fat quid selling Australia's credibility short. Smart-alec galahs like Germaine Greer, Clive James and that old sheila, Dame Edna, who dresses up as a man and tips the bucket on our incomparable cultural attainments in front of the crowned heads of Europe.

> The Australian Government has lashed out and bought a nice old period-style maisonette a stone's throw from prestigious Bloomsville Square with ample parking facilities outside for visiting Australian academics y'know, and post-graduate ponces in their pre-owned, as-new, VW campers. We've given this assignment to you, Les, because you're that smart you could sell soap to the Poms. Rustle up a horny little Yuletide promotional package, get off your campus with your skeleton staff, take a firm grip on your syllabus and stick it up 'em. End of quote, Roxy, and how about a nice juicy steak in the Chips Rafferty executive dining annexe? You look like a girl who could do with something hot inside her. New para.

On another occasion, the publication of *The Best of Parkinson*, Sir Les delivered this acceptably sycophantic 'Ode to Parky':

> If he gets nervous, well, it's never showed
> His face is like a mile of rugged road,
> His crow's-feet are the dried-up beds of smiles
> And all his best friends know that he's got piles
> – Of charm, pazazz and British spunk and phlegm,
> Of TV interviewers he's the gem.
> To make it interesting he could interview a Zulu or Iraqi
> His name is Parky.
>
> This bloke can conjure laughter and applause
> In the wake of Ratbags, Poofs and Crashing Bores.
> And if he's pushed for spicy dialogue
> He'll ask you if you ever nudged the grog.
>
> Australian critics are all chippy guys
> They tried to chop old Parky down to size.
> Some even said: 'Go back where you come from
> – We won't be taught charisma by a Pom.'
> But he knows the average Aussie journalist
> Is following orders, jealous or half-pissed!
>
> He smiles, he does his job, he doesn't care
> When you're the top, where do you go from there?
> So raise your glass of lager, rum or sake
> Whether you be Hun or Nip or Darkie
> And drink the health of my old cobber – PARKY!

When Sir Les was awarded a honorary doctorate by the Cambridge Union in 1983, he celebrated the honour with some 'Cambridge Couplets':

Tonight you have donned your most solemn regalia
To extol the glory of my homeland, Australia
And I, humble son of that continent brown,
Proudly accept this black cap and gown.
And now I've got it on my back
Let no bastard try to get it back!
But what does the average bloke expect
When he visits this shrine of intellect?
A bunch of poofdahs and Brideshead blighters
Shirt-lifters and pommy pillow-biters?
Sure, the girls all love my laid-back Australian style
When I walk past they flash me the vertical smile.
They'd love to join me on a Cambridge punt
For a seminar on Immanuel Kant.
But you're a bonzer bunch of lasses and lads
And I'm real proud to be honoured by youse undergrads,
So, no matter what any bastard sez
When you think of Australia think of old Les
And, with that, gentle ladies, may I now withdraw
And I haven't said THAT to a woman before.

He has written two books: the first, *Les Patterson's Australia*
(1978) is the slighter, an album of captioned pictures
showing Sir Les at work building 'this brown unpleasant land
of Australia' — Patterson, the cultural bureaucrat, the film
producer, the multiculturalist, the environmentalist, the
patron of Aboriginal arts, the student of Bertolt Brecht, the
wine and cheese connoisseur, the media personality. The
second, *The Traveller's Tool* (1985) is a gruesome set of do's
and don'ts for the 'professional adulterer and family man'.
Richard Ingrams described it as '150 pages of pure filth'
made memorable by Patterson's extraordinary, McKenzie-
esque vocabulary. Characteristic of its advice to his fellow-
sots is this: 'A good tip for scallywag drivers like me is to
wake up in the morning and nip out into the drive and check
the front bumper for blood and teeth. It's also not a bad idea

Mrs Everage on her first trip 'overseas' in 1962. (*John Tourrier*)

His London 'satirical' début at the Establishment Club, Greek Street, 1962. (*Lewis Morley*)

Lance Boyle, Australian industrial consultant and committed socialist, at play, 1978. The research assistant on the right is Diane Millstead. (*By courtesy of the* Bulletin, *Sydney*)

Above: At
Salamis,
Cyprus, with
local
inhabitant, on
holiday, 1969.
(*Lewis Morley*)

At the
National
Theatre,
London, with
his third wife,
Diane
Millstead, *circa*
1982.

Dame Edna pioneering marsupial fashions, *circa* 1980.

Self-portrait,
1989. (*From
the collection
of Edward and
Peta Clark,
Golden Crust
Gallery,
Melbourne*)

Below: Sandy
Stone n.d.

Sir Les Patterson in formal attire during a performance of *Peter and the Shark* at the Royal Albert Hall, 1982.

Dame Edna cherishing Australia's embattled native fauna.

With Lizzie Spender after their marriage at Spoleto, Italy, in June 1990.

to check that there isn't any strange sheilah flaked out on the back seat with her scanties around her ankles. Not exactly the sight you want your wife to see when she shuffles out to get the milk.' Sir Les himself, when launching the book in Canberra, said: 'It's full of fantastic stuff . . .and a good deal of bullshit. Frankly I was pissed when I wrote it.'

Sir Les also made in 1987 a disastrous movie, *Les Patterson Saves the World* – a farce about a plot by the fanatical Arab dictator of Abu Nivea to destroy the West by spreading an AIDS-like disease called HELP. With the assistance of Dame Edna ('a kind of Jane Fonda for the eighties' and now a CIA agent), Sir Les ('a cross between Cyril Smith, Monsieur Hulot and Billy Carter' and now Australian ambassador to Abu Nivea) prevents the destruction of a cure, delivers it to US Intelligence and saves the world. Although the film starred Humphries (as Edna and Les), Joan Rivers (as President of USA) and Pamela Stephenson, it was both a critical and a box-office débâcle.

There were several touches of Humphriesian zaniness – a glimpse of a Sydney suburb in which a fat pedestrian in shorts and white socks is walking a tame kangaroo, watched by a group of macho gays, or of the kasbah-like cabin of an Air Niv aeroplane in which camel drivers sleep in luggage racks, a wailing leper begs alms in the aisle and Sir Les swigs his whisky flask as he ogles the seedy belly-dancers doubling as stewardesses. In one scene Arab urchins pelt camel dung at the once dapper chamber music critic of London's *Sunday Times*, now being crucified in the public square for being caught with a pink gin. In another when the huge, greasy Inspector Farouk finds hundreds of pills and capsules in the handbag of an Australian Possum for Peace and threatens her with death for drug-smuggling, Edna protests: 'Valium isn't a drug. It's a food.' But these were not enough to save the film. It ran for a few days and was then withdrawn.

Les Patterson, the heavy drinker, smoker and fornicator, frequently contemplates his death (and even sometimes wonders if he isn't dead already). He remembers that his father died in his sleep 'half-way between the bar and the dunny', and he sings, in country-and-western style, of how he foresees his own passing:

> Well, if you're a travelling man like me,
> Life isn't a bed of roses.
> I'll be found one day on the floor of my suite
> With coronary thrombosis.

There will be, he imagines, the remnants of a Chinese take-away on the bed, the butt of a still burning cigarette, and a frightened hooker who will testify that he collapsed while trying to open the mini-bar.

It is a modern death, Australian and cosmopolitan, and — compared with Sandy Stone's genteel, heart-rending departure while the Harpic cleans the toilet — a sordid one. But it too is moving: the intrepid Les will die as he lived and will go down fighting, a combination of Sir Toby Belch and Apeneck Sweeney.

17

Housewife-Superstar!

When at 11 p.m. on Tuesday 16 March 1976, at the Apollo in Shaftesbury Avenue, Barry Humphries opened his *House-wife-Superstar!* (with the sub-title 'A reasonably amusing show') produced by Michael White, he launched one of the most popular series of one-man shows since Charles Dickens' tours in the 1860s. They have continued every year since, on the stage of English and Australian theatres, cabarets and clubs, with sorties to the United States, New Zealand, Hong Kong and the Gulf states.

His opening at 11 p.m. was in order to distinguish himself from a number of major openings competing with him that week in March, including the Lyttelton in the National Theatre on the South Bank, a Feydeau farce at the Phoenix and a spectacular musical by Melvin Bragg and Tony Hatch at the Prince of Wales (*Plays and Players* did not even list *Housewife-Superstar!*). Humphries' public announcement was that he had chosen 11 p.m. because none of the critics would come anywhere until the pubs closed.

Housewife-Superstar! was as much a party as a show, beginning with the signs in the lobby: 'Australians Normal Prices' and 'Paraplegic Toilets 8th Floor. Please Use Stairs' and ending with the orgy of gladdie-waving as the theatre filled with large coloured balloons tumbling from the ceiling. Les Patterson, staggering down the aisle, whisky in hand, to the stage made his sensational if malodorous début introducing Dame Edna:

Before we drag up the curtain on this evening's superlative entertainment permit me to introduce myself to you good people if I may. My name is Les Patterson. P-A-T-T-E-R-S-O-N. And I have the honour to be the Australian Cultural Attaché to the Court of St James's. I also front up our Fine Arts Task Force here in Europe.

Now I am not going to insult your intelligence here tonight, ladies and gentlemen, by pretending that I haven't had a drink, because I have. I've had a couple of drinks. Who hasn't, for Christ's sake! But I'm not full, ladies and gentlemen. *I am not full.* And I'd be a mug if I tried to pretend to you good people that I know all the ropes and ins and outs of the culture racket. To be perfectly honest with you I am still feeling my way around, as a couple of delightfully built little sheilahs out there in the foyer will no doubt confirm. But you know, in my capacity as Cultural Attaché to the Court of St James's I meet all kinds and I bump into a lot of expatriates, but strangely enough it's the Australian ex-pat that really gives me the toms. I refer of course to the long-haired plum-in-the-mouth élitist variety who come over here and turn a quid by knocking their homeland. You all know the sort who depict their fellow Australians as a bunch of ockers, piss-artists and foul-mouthed beer-swilling Bazza McPhersons. These knockers, in my book, are lower than the basic wage, ladies and gentlemen. They're as low as a snake's armpits. If I run into any of my fellow Australians rubbishing their homeland and knocking our famous finesse and refinement I'll kick his teeth so far down his throat he'll have to stick his toothbrush up his freckle to clean them. Because I am here to tell you we've got culture in Australia, ladies and gentlemen. We've got culture up to our *arseholes*! As they say in the classics, 'Arse Vita Longa Brevis'. Not art for art's sake but art for Christ's sake.

Oh, cripes, oh gees, I have had a few. I'm sorry, ladies and gentlemen. I'm as full as a Catholic school. I'm as full as a bull's bum. So I'm going to sit down and let this unique reflection of our attainments and incomparable life-style get under way and who better to kick off than Dame Edna Everage herself. So without any further ado I'd like you all to give her a warm hand on her opening and give her the clap she so richly deserves. (*Exit unsteadily, beaming.*)

Dame Edna, in a denim two-piece and blue tights, immediately injected the note of tension, the odour of sulphur, which became her hallmark: 'There are some critics here tonight. Stand up, boys, so we can look at you.' ('Did your intrepid correspondent obey'? asked Benedict Nightingale. 'Did he hell! We all played the coward.') Then turning back to her guests, she followed her established, unscripted 'routine' and began chatting with individual possums – Fibber (who claimed to know Edna's daughter), Senior (who was, Edna said, drugged for his evening's leave from the twilight home), Gobbler (noisily eating his sweets) or Noddy (dozing off); discussing bathrooms ('The tiles, Judy! What colour are the tiles?); reprimanding: 'Behave yourselves or I'll keep you all in!' ... 'Look at me when I'm talking to you, woman!' ... 'What's the matter? Haven't you ever sat in a West End theatre at midnight and heard a lady describe her bathroom before?'; exchanging confidences ('My husband has never seen me naked, nor has he expressed the least desire to do so.'); berating her trendy daughter-in-law, Joyleen in her Ruislip pad, a converted warehouse (where her razor had hairs of various colours in it); smothering her dress-designer son, Kenny, the winner of the Mr Leather Competition; airing her prejudices ('Words mean nothing to tinted people, but they love bright colours', she explained, waving a scarlet chiffon scarf at a bemused Pakistani); and shrieking, 'I'm just a silly woman' as she conducted the gladdie finale. It was all, Edna said, a nice change from *The Seagull*, playing next door with Joan Plowright.

The audience spilling out into the street afterwards looked, one reporter said, 'like the proverbial stunned mullet'. The critics were excited. Michael Billington found Humphries 'extravagantly funny'; Julian Jebb called him 'the funniest man alive'; John Osborne believed that his genius had created something that was not there before – an Australia which is as real as Cobbett's England or Trollope's Barchester, a nightmare land which has its tally throughout the modern world. John Elsom said the performance changed one's life: ' . . . it makes us think and feel differently afterwards'. Jack Tinker, in his selection for the *Plays and Players'* annual awards for best plays, actors, directors etc of 1976 declared: 'My first inclination was to nominate Dame Edna Everage and her *éminence gris*, Mr Barry Humphries, for every award.' Harold Hobson, who had brushed aside *Just a Show* in 1969 and ignored *Housewife-Superstar!* when it opened in March at the Apollo, announced in May when it moved to the Globe: 'He is a wonder, a glory and a terror. Do not miss him.' (Julian Jebb thought that, in the years since 1969, Humphries' art had broadened and deepened. 'The words are funnier, the jokes more perfectly timed, the observation is more hair raisingly meticulous.') As for Edna, Billington found her a 'marvellously monstrous creation'; Elsom 'a superb comic creation'; and Ned Chaillet ranked her with the characters of George Allen and Jack Benny as 'one of the lasting comic inventions'.

The show ran to packed houses for four months (at the Apollo and then at the Globe) and almost 500,000 people saw it. Dame Edna was now indeed famous: at Royal Ascot in a hat modelled on the Sydney Opera House, she received more publicity than the Queen, and she never looked back. At the time Humphries described 1976 as 'the happiest year I have known'. Only America was able to resist Edna. After playing the Revd Strachey in Bruce Beresford's Australian movie *The Getting of Wisdom*, Humphries opened *House-*

wife-Superstar! (again produced by Michael White) to an enthusiastic audience in the small Theatre Four on West 55th Street in October 1977. 'Lowbrow Entertainment at Last', announced one placard and 'Minorities Are Welcome Up to a Point', declared another, while those needing Braille programmes were advised: 'Try Seeing the Manager.' A map of the notorious Koala Triangle was also exhibited in the foyer. Les Patterson, now Australian Cultural Attaché to the United Nations, in an electric-blue suit with an orange shirt, sloshing his glass of whisky, and slobbering over the orchestra, introduced Dame Edna who proceeded to grill the audience about their bathrooms and confided in them: 'I've learned to love the Japanese by thinking of them as Caucasian dwarfs with hepatitis'; 'That man next to you darling, his suit fits him like a glove, it sticks out in five places'; 'The Lincoln Center – where Abraham Lincoln was assassinated.'

The audience was, as Rex Reed put it in the *Daily News*, reduced to 'a state of helplessness, howling at everything', and at the traditional first-night party at Sardi's, a delighted Stephen Sondheim was certain that the show would play New York for years. 'But in another room,' Humphries said, 'I found the management huddled gloomily over early copies of the *New York Times* whose new theatre critic Richard Eder had branded the show as "abysmal". They went on looking gloomy and said we were doomed.' The show, Richard Eder wrote, 'gives new depths to the phrase "Down Under". Mr Humphries' efforts to be funny for nearly two hours reportedly were very successful in London. It is hard to imagine why. Perhaps Londoners, who tend to judge Australians as noisy and uncultured beer-drinkers, found nourishment for their prejudices. It may be that busloads of spectators rolled in from Nuneaton and Nottingham to the West End. Here in New York a crosstown bus trip seems excessive.'

Some critics did not follow the *New York Times*. Rex Reed

called the show 'a banquet of madness, energy and just plain fun, a wild uproarious entertainment'. Andy Warhol in the *Village Voice* wrote that 'no one can afford to pass up this assault of lunacy'. Howard Kessel in *Women's Wear Daily* enjoyed 'the daffiness of it, the inspired silliness'. But the *New York Times* malediction set the tone. Edith Oliver in the *New Yorker* found the jokes 'awful' and Dame Edna 'a bore'. *News World* concluded: 'like litter on 42nd Street, it is something worth missing'. The *New York Post* referred to 'a patently pointless evening with all the redeeming social value of a case of mumps'. One Australian correspondent summed it up: 'Australia's First Lady has gone down on Broadway as a jaffa might descend a lift-well at the Empire State Building' (lines Humphries was to use as copy).

This was an exaggeration. The show ran for four weeks – at a time when several shows opened and closed within days. But compared with London's four months it was a sour disappointment and the contempt of so many critics was hurtful: all Humphries could do was to ridicule the *New York Times* and its temporary critic, as he did at each performance and complain to Andy Warhol in the *Village Voice*: 'He was until recently foreign correspondent to Madrid and is probably accustomed to bull fights, is new to the job, is *terribly* anxious to please, wants to be sort of fashionably scathing and has something like five to seven children and a clubfoot . . .' But, as Humphries said, the *New York Times* has the power.

Part of the problem was the trans-Atlantic cultural gulf. 'As soon as I got on stage,' Humphries said later, 'I realized why it was that comedians like Spike Milligan had never played New York ...The fact that they speak English is about the only thing they have in common with us.' There was also the popular American distrust of female impersonators and transvestism. Humphries is not a traditional female impersonator. Dame Edna is not a drag act. She does not mime, as Humphries put it, to recordings of Liza Minnelli. She is a created character to be acted like any other. But this was not how Americans saw it in 1977. Above all there had been no conditioning of the New York public for what it was about to see, nothing comparable to the years of perform-ances, successes and setbacks that had characterized Hum-phries' career in London since 1959. He arrived in New York as if out of the blue. Only a few friends – English, American, Australian – knew him, and while the press reported that the artist Diane Millstead (whom he was soon to marry) and he made 'an eye-catching couple', even in Manhattan, this was not enough to overcome public indifference.

Since then Humphries has made only a few attempts to reach Americans, including some television appearances on a short-lived Joan Rivers Late Show in 1986. But America's turn must surely come: Dame Edna has declared that she feels that basically she is a New York Intellectual.

Meanwhile in England and Australia Barry Humphries continued to attract larger – and younger – audiences, as the Dame Edna and Sir Les duo grew more outrageous and as other characters from the Humphries' family – the suburban Sandy Stone, the corrupt union leader Lance Boyle, the trendy Rev Roger A. Nunn shared the stage. In 1978–9 the next one-man show, called *Isn't It Pathetic At His Age* in Australia, produced by Malcolm C. Cooke and Hayden Price, and *A Night with Dame Edna* in England, produced by Bethall Reynolds, ran for months in both countries. In Australia its subtitle was 'The most out-of-touch show in town' – a reference to his critics who continued to ignore the packed houses and find him 'passé' or 'burnt out'.

Les Patterson again began the party:

I'm a maverick, I'm a wag, I'm a hard-nosed carpet-bagging trouble-shooter and if ever there's any strife in the world that needs a bit of *finesse*, a little *savoir-faire* – what has become known in diplomatic circles as 'the Patterson touch' — they send for old Les. I'm a sort of Australian Henry Kissinger.

But I have to do a lot of entertaining in my job: I've always got me hand in me slush fund. And in my job as diplomat I meet people who've never met an Australian before. And, you know, it's a marvellous feeling to know that they judge by *me*! It gives me a lovely warm feeling deep down where it really counts.

Sandy Stone, deceased (he had died in an earlier show while the Harpic was cleansing), now reappeared to describe his meagre funeral service:

Needless to say there wasn't much of a turn-up at the funeral. My wife must have a bit of Scotch blood in her because she got a few quotes on me first — she put out tenders — but in the end she settled for a very reasonable little local firm of funeral directors. Nice vehicle too — burgundy, power steering, though I think they could have Hoovered out the back seat. My poor little widow had to go all the way out to the crematorium up to her ankles in confetti! Blessed ethnic driver too — a man doesn't want a Greek at the wheel on his last trip and they don't go at the reverential pace that we're used to here — forty miles an hour through two amber lights and a cripples' crossing. I wasn't so concerned for myself naturally, but if Beryl hadn't had her seatbelt on it could have been a double event.

Beryl's a marvellous little person though. There she was — sitting in the back seat of the cortège whizzing out to the cremmie, her plate full and her cup of grief running over, but she still had the presence of mind to get the driver to pull over outside our local jeweller so she could drop off my watch to get the wristband shortened. Not many women would have thought of that.

In accordance with Beryl's tasteful request there weren't too many out there to see me off. There was only Beryl. And me up to a point. Oh, and Thelma Bullock and the Longmires. And the Nettletons without their kiddies. And Valda – dear Valda Clissold – she was there, bless her heart, a *true* Clissold. And she was terribly upset too, underneath, in all probability. And there was Nurse Younghusband, and Greg Younghusband, Nurse Younghusband's young husband. And there were three very distressed people at the back of the chapel. I've never seen more distressed-looking people in my life. Turned out they were waiting for the nine forty-five service – still it was very nice of them to put their heads around the corner. They were not called upon to do so.

At the wake, Beryl offered Sandy's effects to friends and neighbours who clustered like flies around a honey-pot, but after a good deal of humming and ha-ing, they went home empty-handed. Meanwhile Sandy's ashes remain at the Garden of Rest which Beryl sometimes visits. 'I don't know how long she'll keep that up. It's a long haul out to the Necropolis to view my niche ... and they've bunged my urn so high up the wall, you'd need an extension ladder to pay your respects.'

New characters presented included the left-wing trade union boss of a building industry union, Lance Boyle, in Hong Kong on a Churchill Fellowship. Telephoning his research assistant in Sydney, he plans industrial retaliation for not having been upgraded to first-class on his Qantas flight and for not having luxury accommodation in his hotel. Then he learns of a threat to his American tour:

What? What's that? Why didn't you tell me this before, Lee? Why didn't you tell me this before? They've pulled the men off what? They have pulled the men off the big new Yankee satellite tracking station outside Albury?

They can't do that. How did they do it? Don't tell me. I
know how they done it. It turns out it's on a sacred tribal
site, am I right? How did I guess that one? It's the oldest
trick in the book. I've pulled it a dozen times myself. I
know how they fix it. They flew in a mob of Abos, didn't
they? They slipped them a case of Penfold's Royal
Reserve, didn't they?

The men have got to go back. I promised the PM that
job would be OK. I had meaningful discussions with the
Prime bloody Minister. He told the Yanks it would be
sweet and when I get to the States the Yanks were going to
give me an air-conditioned Buick with unlimited mileage
and a free trip round Disneyland with a double ride on
Space Mountain. Now that's up shit creek I suppose. I'm
wasting my time in this dump. I should be back in Sydney.
I know who's behind this. It's those mongrels from the
Victorian Branch. They've always hated me, those scum.
They've always hated the intellectuals in the party. They'll
be voting next.

Humphries commented that Lance Boyle is as delightful to
act as he is repulsive to watch. He amused himself, while
doing the act, by scanning the stalls and picking out 'the
pious pinkos'. 'Their poor little pinched faces fell most
entertainingly when they realized that the odious operator
on the boards was one of their own sacrosanct, self-
sacrificing trade union lefties.'

In the second half, Dame Edna, now the 'thinking man's
Eva Peron' in a 'raunchy, zappy' tennis frock and frizzy wig,
delivered ninety minutes of insults and innuendoes. 'Poor
Norm, his prostate has hung over me for years'; 'When
Charlie Chaplin vanished from his grave, it was almost
certainly to tour Australia'; 'What a cunning little linguist
you are'; 'What an interesting person you probably are';
'What are you doing with that handkerchief? Got a little
discharge, have you?' She closed the party with the orgy of

gladioli-pelting and thrusting as she squawked: 'I hope you can keep it up as long as I can at my age.'

The theatre critics were almost unanimous. In London, Sheridan Morley placed Dame Edna among the top creations of the century, along with Harold Lloyd's student, Chaplin's tramp and Hancock's loser. John Barber called Humphries 'the greatest music-hall artist surviving into modern times'. Michael Billington thought that only Ken Dodd could rival the 'sense of orgiastic delight' which Humphries created, and the Society of West End Theatre Awards chose the show as the best comedy performance of the year. The critics also began to discern the furious indignation that fuelled Humphries' comedy. In England Billington called him a vaudeville Swift, using disgust as a comic weapon; Morley found a 'naked loathing' eerily mixed with the showbiz enthusiasm of gladdie-hurling; and Polly Toynbee (whose father Philip had turned bell, book and candle against Humphries' book *Bizarre* in 1965) said he combined a drag act of genius with the venom and passion of a true satirist. In Australia H.G. Kippax saw him as a moralist sternly using laughter as a purgative, while Katherine Brisbane found that 'the root of Humphries' genius' is the moral disturbance he creates. Inevitably Humphries had by now attracted a legion of hostile critics, especially in Australia, but Edna's status and fame were unchallengeable. At an Amnesty International's *The Secret Policeman's Other Ball*, she sang exultantly:

> The royal visitors who call;
> A concert in the Albert Hall;
> That's what my public means to me.
> All those requests I get to stay
> With famous folk in St Tropez,
> That's their idea of fun for me.
> But you can keep Roman Polanski and Bianca,
> It's for the company of nobodies like you I hanker.

> You're my shelter from the storm,
> You're as precious as my Norm.
> That's what my public means to me.

As her innuendoes and bathroom jokes grew cruder, her
compassion for cripples or lepers crueller, her fashions
grosser, her culture coarser, her politics trendier she was
becoming the very paradigm of the age.

It was at this time in June 1979, after the end of the London
run of *A Night with Dame Edna* and before Humphries took
it to those cities in Australia which earlier had missed the
Australian version, *Isn't It Pathetic*, he and Diane Millstead
were married at the Marylebone Register Office, with a
service of blessing at St James's, Piccadilly, the parish church
of the Royal Academy. Their friends who attended included
Joan Bakewell, Sir John Betjeman, Sir John Rothenstein, John
Wells, Ian Davidson (his director), Nicholas Garland, and
Madeleine Orr (who was the first Madge Allsop and was
shortly to die of cancer). Diane included gladdies in her
bouquet at the church and Humphries wore a gladdie
brooch. The marriage was to last ten years.

18

Megastar

Interviewed late in 1981 for the department of oral history at the National Library of Australia, Barry Humphries cheerfully declared: 'Nineteen eighty-one has been the most successful and indeed the happiest year that I've had, professionally ... I'm in the best health,. I feel, that I've ever been in ... I have regular medical checkups and apparently I'm very fit, and that's good because for a long time I wasn't. I've had my health crisis and I like to think that's behind me and I'm going to go on from strength to strength.' He repeated: 'It's a great year.'

Nineteen eighty-one was indeed an extraordinary year. His son Oscar was born in April (and his second son, Rupert, in October the following year). He published an anthology of his more tightly scripted sketches (that is, excluding Edna's ad-libbed badinage), *A Nice Night's Entertainment*, dedicated to his wife Diane Millstead; the Australian authorities accepted a recommendation to have him appointed a member of the Order of Australia; and he received a standing ovation at a Melbourne Grammar Old Boys' dinner at which he delivered his bitter-sweet poem about his old school:

> Remember Bully Taylor's classroom, desks deep-furrowed
>   and engraved,
> And carbolic scented boarders, half-neglected, half-
>   depraved,

The swarming Quad, the physics Lab — which smelt of
  hard-boiled eggs —
A visit to the library to view Miss Elliott's legs.
The Assembly where some fainted — or else vaguely lost
  control —
As we sang a rousing ditty begging with our heart and soul
That something called 'a Dark Blue Twenty' would please
  make the leather roll!

Where are they now — the prefects? Stripped of their
  awesome powers.
Do they miss their footy comrades in the Lifebuoy-
  scented showers?
Do they long to cane a slacker or humiliate a shirk
As they Volvo down to Portsea leaving Judy with the
  Merc?
They don't miss English literature or algebra or sums,
But as middle age envelops them, a poignant feeling
  comes
When, with thumping heart, they recollect those tight
  blue schoolboy bums.

But above all 1981 was the year in which, now represented
by Dennis Smith, he launched his show *An Evening's
Intercourse with Barry Humphries* which filled his largest
theatres yet, including the Theatre Royal, Drury Lane, for
ten weeks.

Shortly before the show opened Humphries appeared in
three spots on the *Parkinson Show*, first as Barry Humphries
('For a very long time, Australia was a very peculiar and
remote place to the British public, and I perhaps flatter
myself that I may have been instrumental in towing it, if not
as close as the Isle of Wight, almost as close ...I wanted to
demonstrate that Australia is a funny place'); then as Sir Les
Patterson ('What is the image that I am bloody successful in
projecting? That of Australia as a thinking organism. It's

bloody fantastic the publicity we're getting, largely due to the efforts of my good self. You know it wasn't many moons ago that they thought we were a bunch of rough diamonds down under, but you know we've got more culture than a penicillin factory. No worries.') and finally as Dame Edna ('I think I'm the acceptable face of feminism. I'm the feminine face of feminism if you like'):

> My daughter Valmai is giving me a lot of worry. She had a little shoplifting experience. Oh yes, and of course she modelled herself a little bit on Patti Hearst too. She held up a bank the other day. It wasn't in the news here. I had Margaret [Whitlam] stop it as a matter of fact. She held up a sperm bank as a matter of fact. She wants to be a one-parent family. The secret cameras got her. Can you imagine looking at the paper one morning and seeing your own daughter with a little rifle and sawn-off shotgun and people throwing test tubes at her. I don't know who she was looking for but there was a rumour Warren Beatty had made a deposit.

The press reported that after *The Parkinson Show* appearances the switchboard at the Theatre Royal, Drury Lane, was jammed for days.

As further pre-publicity Sir Les Patterson delivered his 'Poetic Address to the Press':

> So kindly I beg you good folk raise thy glass.
> This show is a much-needed shot in the arse.
> But before you all rush back to your brewers
> A word of advice to theatre reviewers.
> Make sure you don't give Dame Edna a stinker
> Or she'll rip off your balls like she done with Jack Tinker.*

*The distinguished critic of the *Daily Mail* who had once, imprudently, given Humphries an equivocal review.

Signs in the theatre foyer advised: 'Arabs use dunnies please', and 'The management regrets material offensive to bus drivers, full dykes, pinkos, poofs, pigs, wogs, chiropractors, bigots, Micks and (in Australia) *National Times* feature writers.' Inside, *Oklahoma* was played in German. As the lights dimmed in the haunted Drury Lane, a recorded voice (Charles Osborne's) advised patrons that any malign supernatural manifestations would be dealt with by the 'fully qualified exorcists stationed throughout this auditorium'. One new character appeared – the barefoot and bald Phil Philby, who had just won the Golden Goanna award for his film *Cage of Darkness*, the first of 'an eight-part trilogy about anti-lesbian discrimination in an Aboriginal women's prison'. Lance Boyle, on the phone to his secretary, plans an Arab lunch:

Listen, Lee, for the last time. It's a top secret mission by a group of Baghdad businessmen. Don't call them shepherds. And they are not 'tea-towel heads'. We're looking here at petro-dollars, so don't knock it. Who do you think paid for this new place of mine? How come the union can afford to occupy a five-storey Besser brick office block in the inner city? The dues didn't pay that lot. *Union* dues, Leone.

These men have a genuine interest in our country and its resources. They might look a bit shonky, but they're prepared to invest big bickies in upgrading the Arab image over here. Why do you think every stringer-journo from the Melbourne *Age* to the Cairns *Chronicle* has had a freebie to Baghdad and Tripoli? The Poms aren't too proud to let them in. At the hotels in London they can park their Benz in the foyers and shit in the lifts.

Sandy Stone reported that Clarrie Lockwood, who had 'had his eye on Beryl's kumquat for years', finally married her. They sold 36 Gallipoli Crescent and moved north to a condo on the Gold Coast. Before leaving they found an old family album with 'faded snaps the colour of tea that you made with condensed milk'. It was damp and crawling with lice, and Clarrie carried it to the incinerator on his shovel. 'It was a beggar to burn; a tin of kero didn't do it. He (Clarrie) had to delve into the incinerator with a garden fork, turning the pages and sticking them through . . . 1936 . . . 1937 . . . 1938 . . .'

Dame Edna, now in a gold-trimmed romper suit, held a barbecue on stage for selected guests ('You look,' she confided to one woman, a leading journalist, 'as if you need something hot inside you'), and she produced a shoe-net to collect shoes which she would analyse before offering counsel. ('This isn't a shoe – it's a cry for help.') Her possums were brought up-to-date with her unfolding family saga. Her mother has been frog-marched off to the Sylvia Plath suite in a geriatric unit and her personal 'things' burnt ('I couldn't help but laugh'); her husband, 'prostrate with his prostate', is dying; her son Kenny tried to confess his homosexuality to her shortly after she had taken her 'moggies' ('I'm hilarious, Mum,' she thought she remembered him saying, and she replied, 'Kenny, I am too!' 'What!' You mean with Madge?!' But Edna had fallen asleep); her daughter Valmai, once a sexual options counsellor, is now a Trotskyist (and bank robber); her trendy daughter-in-law Joyleen continues to resist Edna's attempt to destroy her marriage; and Madge Allsop, her widowed bridesmaid, bisexual companion and punching bag ('I feel like some fladge. Come here Madge') ordered a Joan Crawford face-lift, but got a Broderick Crawford by mistake ('It was the shortest operation in the history of cosmetic surgery') and sits on stage bandaged like a mummy.

The critics were again enthusiastic. In London Michael Billington welcomed the quality of outrage and the whiff of sulphur which have 'almost departed from an age of anaemic comic conformity'. Michael Coveney called Edna 'a modern

marvel' and Sheridan Morley wrote of her 'new heights of
wonder'. (James Fenton's critique was headed 'Dame Edna:
a burnt-out star.') In Australia the leading critics, like the
audiences, were equally enthusiastic, although the *National
Times* found a stink of fear and loathing in Humphries'
'profoundly reactionary art', and a leftist literary magazine
ran a sketch by a prominent Australian subsidized playwright presenting Humphries as blindly prejudiced against
the working class.

These censors were encouraged by the wide, almost
unanimous, critical dismissal in both England and Australia,
of Humphries' next show, *Last Night of the Poms* (September
1981 in London) or *Song of Australia* (February 1983 in
Sydney and Melbourne.) An entirely new departure – and a
collaboration with the American composer-conductor, Carl
Davis – it was 'one of the most difficult shows I have done'.
The first half was an 'Overture with Australian Themes',
recalling several colonial worksongs, shanties and laments
and ending with 'Waltzing Matilda' against a landscape of
abandoned billycarts, dying trees, deserted tucker boxes and
desert dingoes. (Julian Jebb, one of the few enthusiastic
critics: 'Mr Humphries is in a ferment of creation,' found
'Waltzing Matilda' 'ravishingly orchestrated' and the overture
'delicate and robust' with a right to enter the repertoire on
the level of, say Constant Lambert's *Rio Grande*.) This was
followed by Sir Les Patterson, backed by the orchestra,
reading *Peter and the Shark*, a parody of Prokofiev's *Peter and
the Wolf*, with Peter as a bronzed surfer, the bird a laughing
kookaburra, the duck a platypus, the cat a dingo and
Grandfather 'Beachcomber Bill'. The opening lines are:

> Early one December morning Peter strapped his Austra-
> lian-made hand-crafted fibreglass surf-board to the back of
> his moke and hammered down the Anzac freeway to
> lonely Effluent Beach where the big bomboras break.

As Carl Davis wrote: 'Roll over, Serge Prokofiev.'

In the second half Dame Edna leads the presentation of the nine cantos of *Song of Australia*, a 'profane' cantata which traces the history of Australia from the primordial gloom through the age of British settlement (the refrain 'Australia must at all costs be British' is accompanied by an extended Laughing Chorus) on to the glorious Age of Edna.

Humphries was flogging a dead kangaroo, said Jack Tinker in London. A grotesquely overblown joke, said Irving Wardle. An expensive mistake, said Nicholas de Jongh. An uneasy evening which misuses Humphries' talents, said Anthony Thorncroft. In Australia John Moses called it 'pedestrian' and 'grandiloquent self-indulgence'; Bob Crimeen said, 'Barry has bombed' and Richard Le Moignan's review, which found the show 'disappointing' was headed 'The rise and fall of Dame Edna Everage!'

Yet, despite the critics, the cantata was a huge popular hit. Humphries (and Carl Davis) packed the cavernous Albert Hall in London, the Regent Theatre in Sydney and the Melbourne Concert Hall. Millions watching the show on television experienced the amazing spectacle of a packed 'Alfred' Hall, singing, with full orchestra and choir, the Dadaist hymn, in the Cantata's tumultuous conclusion:

Audience:	Why do we love Australia?
	Why does it haunt us still?
	There's nobody we know there,
	And it costs so much to go there,
	The chances are we never will.
	But still we all love Australia
	Whatever Australia may be
Dame Edna:	It's the land of milk and honey
	It's so rich . . . and safe . . . and funny.
Audience:	Australia you're the land for me.

For the Australian season, there were some variations. For example:

Why do we love Australia?
Why does it haunt us still?
We've got so much on our plate here,
The world wants to emigrate here,
And one day I'm afraid they will.
But *still* we all love Australia
Whatever Australia may be.
Let our voices swell with pride.
We are extremely satisfied.
Australia you're the land for me.

19

Icon

Barry Humphries returned triumphantly to the familiar format of his one-man shows with his next production, called *Tears Before Bedtime* in Australia and *Back with a Vengeance* in London. If this show convinced Sheridan Morley that only several teams of highly trained psychiatrists could fathom the British obsession with this actor-writer who 'looks like a myopic fairy godmother from a nightmare by Fellini', Paul Taylor was satisfied that Humphries is simply 'the greatest comic entertainer of our time'.

Before opening at the Strand (not just a theatre but 'England's preferred Community Entertainment Option') in November 1987, Humphries launched the television series, a Dadaist chat-show called *The Dame Edna Experience*. 'Other chat shows,' Edna explained, 'choose nonentities to interview celebrities, so for the first time you will see celebrities talking to their peer.' There was also a uniformed registered nurse on standby, a big band, a vast staircase, identification badges for the guests in case Edna forgot their names, and an ejector button to expel backwards anyone she found boring – for example, the singer Cliff Richard on the first show. Madge, played by Emily Perry, now came into her own as Edna's cowed, silent but always adoring companion. Although the guests were usually not permitted to say very much – this chat-show was a monologue occasionally interrupted by strangers – and were definitely not permitted to promote their special interest, books, films or plays, eighteen were found for the six shows of 1987 prepared to risk humiliation, looking as if they were jollying their way (as Martin Cropper put it) through 'a nightmare charity event'.

They included the actress Jane Seymour ('Tell me, Jane, you've been successfully married three times. What's the secret of your success?'), the actor Charlton Heston ('Tell me what you do for a living, Chuck. Haven't I seen you on a chariot?'), the singer Nana Mouskouri (who sang 'When Grecian eyes are smiling through a pair of plastic frames'), the politician-novelist-dramatist Jeffrey Archer (who was ejected or 'aborted' when he began to outline the plot of his new play) and Rudolph Nureyev (with whom she danced!).

The full zaniness of it was caught in a later programme when Jane Fonda called from outside on the video phone. 'It's Jane. Will you buzz me in?' she said. 'Jane who?' 'Jane Fonda'. 'What's that you're wearing, possum?' 'I can't believe this. Grey flannel designer jogging clothes.' 'We have a dress code here, Jane. Come again when you've got a nice frock on.' But Jane Fonda, an advertised guest, then climbed the steep flights of stairs to the 33rd floor, where she entered Dame Edna's apartment to see the rock 'n' roll singer Chubby Checker, supported by a band, not only leading a frenzied Dame Edna but also Douglas Fairbanks Jr. and Ronald Reagan Jr. in dancing the Twist. For a moment an open-mouthed Jane Fonda stared silently at this scene from a madhouse, then, half-smiling incredulously, turned her back and quickly walked out. Douglas Fairbanks Jr. later wrote to Humphries: 'What a really fine artist you are. It is so refreshing to have a great reputation like yours confirmed by personal experience.'

The 1987 series may have been a chat-show to kill off chat-shows, but it was a glittering curtain-raiser for the stage show. Outside the Strand theatre, posters proclaimed: 'Late-comers more then welcome', and 'Heart sufferers by-pass this theatre'. Inside, the characteristic Dada note was struck by announcements in Arabic followed by the singing of 'Rock Around the Clock' in Cantonese. Opening the show Sir Les, drunk, beer-stained, supported by Cuban heels, ' the acceptable face of Australian socialism', picked his nose, salivated the front rows, insulted patrons ('her mouth is so large she could suck-start a Harley-Davidson') and once more invited the audience to give Dame Edna the clap she so richly deserved. (It was, Michael Ratcliffe reported, as if the music-hall had never been away.) He was followed by Lance Boyle, now only one step ahead of 'the three-letter men', the tax men:

'Bail! What do you mean I'm on bail? I'm on holidays! I don't like that word, Leon. It is counter-productive. It is not a correct assessment of the situation as it currently stands at the present period of time. I'm surprised to hear my own solicitor subscribing to that cynically orchestrated campaign by the muck-making Moguls of the Media. So you watch your mouth, son. Is that what I pay you three grand a morning for?'

Then came Sandy Stone's most moving, melancholy sketch, 'Sandy Comes Home', about the passing or multicul-turalizing of his doomed English-Australian suburb, Glen Iris. The new, Greek owners of his old home have also, coincidentally, bought Sandy's armchair (with his ghost in it) from the opportunity shop, and he now summed up the changes in his neighbourhood as the 'delightful multi-cultural ethnic minorities' with new ideas displacing the enfeebled old-timers.

Vietnamese bought the Stubbings' house (you could smell their cooking on the bowling green), and Sicilians bought the Littlejohns' (and covered their garden with plastic and pebbles: whenever some snowdrops, hyacinths or jonquils squeezed through, Reno mowed them down 'until they finally gave up').

A daughter-in-law has placed the senile Dot Smith in a nursing home which turned out to have been her childhood home almost seventy years before, with the old summer-house and most of the trees and shrubs removed as part of 'the improvements'. Coming out of sedation Dot recognized, in the doctors' car park, the old peppercorn tree where her Dad had once fixed up a swing; she kept looking at it muttering, 'Where's my swing?', and the Sri Lankan nurse (who liked a Maxwell House and a king-sized mentholated St Moritz with the physio at eleven), quipped: 'She thinks she's a budgie'.

Sandy was, however, grateful that the new owners of his house were keeping some of his old memorabilia, especially his old wedding photograph, which Beryl had forgotten to take with her, and a lock of his mother's hair in a cigarette tin. 'This is my Dreamtime. This is my Sacred Site.' The sketch ended when young Mrs Papadopoulos entered with brush and broom and hurled all the memorabilia into the garbage bin. In this elegy Sandy overpowers even Edna who has long since joined the new barbarians.

One Australian critic, Bob Ellis, wrote: 'I know of no better statement of our nation's fate, the fate of our tribe, than this,' and the writer David Malouf, of both English and Lebanese stock, described it as 'not a sketch but a classic monologue'. The English critics, who despite the enthusiasm of John Betjeman, Jonathan Miller and Julian Jebb almost thirty years earlier, had been slow to respond to Sandy Stone's repeated appearances on the London and provincial stage, now began to see 'dear old Sandy', as John Betjeman, who knew his lines by heart, put it, as a sort of Englishman. He is, Betjeman wrote, 'a very kind man with no taste and much sensibility' who 'demonstrates that underneath the roughest Australians are Londoners and not even Scots or Irish, and they have the full humour of the English music-hall.'

On the other hand Michael Ratcliffe, who once found Sandy so sentimental that 'you didn't know where to look', now found that Sandy was a figure akin, as Michael Ratcliffe observed in 1987, to those who shelter from the wind in Alan Bennett's Morecambe Bay or watch the corner store slowly fill with chapatis and okra in Tony Harrison's Leeds. Francis King noted a 'Chekhovian melancholy' in Sandy's 'touching threnody' and Sir Alec Guinness was 'lost in admiration'.

But Sandy was only the lull before the storm. In the second act Dame Edna erupted, dressed briefly in mourning black for her husband Norm who had just 'been gathered'. He had ticked a donor card (liver, kidneys etc) thinking it was a lunch menu and by the time Edna reached his bedside he was 'only a dent in the pillow'. Her doctor had told her that only time would heal – and he had been absolutely right: it had been at least four hours! Now fully recovered, and transferred into a red party frock and mauve wig, she proceeded to bait the audience in the familiar if inexhaustible way. She should be quoted at length:

I'm redecorating now and I need input. I need new ideas. What colour is your bedroom, Fay darling? Beige, oh, lovely. Presumably a nice shade of beige, is it? Beige walls, are they, Fay? Are they papered or painted? Painted, lovely. A matt or a gloss finish? What, darling? A matt beige. Oh lovely. And do you have a double bed, Fay? Do you? Oh, you're an optimist anyway, Fay. And curtains, what colour? Cream. No windows, but curtains, that's unusual ... But the curtains are very different, aren't they? They need to be, because you might just try to put your head out the window and you'd bash your head against the wall. You look as though you might have done that a few times too. However, what type of carpet do you have, Fay? Fay? A green carpet. Is it a deep green, or a pale green, Fay? A pale green. Is it a Wilton, a berber or shag, Fay? It's a Wilton. I'm glad because frankly I don't like a shag in a bedroom, I don't. What is the matter with you people? You're overtired, you're over-excited.

Now, Fay, do you have an *en suite* bathroom, Fay? No, well a walk never hurt anyone, Fay. Oh Fay, I'm fond of you. You're lovely. That fabric, it's absolutely adorable, isn't it? You were lucky to get so much of it, Fay.

You're going to love Fay when she's on stage in a minute. You are. Fay has gone pale green now ... not yet, Fay, but soon. So soon, that if I was you I would start tensing up now. You wouldn't be alone anyway, Fay. Matthew and Linda will be up here. They will. Matthew and Linda. Out late-comers. They'll be up here writing their essays why we were late.

Did you see my bridesmaid here a little while ago, did you, Fay? Madge ... she's a worry. She was my bridesmaid. She caught my bouquet. On the back of the neck as it happened. I wiped out an entire nerve centre and she has been dependent on me ever since. Well, she's a New Zealander. Have you ever been in a disabled toilet, Fay? Have you? Ever had a peep in one? It's another world in there, it is. It's like a gymnasium in there, it is. Expect to see people doing aerobics, you do. And there's a chrome ladder going up the wall. What do they *do* in there? They spin in, they snip the door, and shin up the wall. That's what they do. And they peep over at us. I'm sure that they do. And I mean this lovingly. I do. I mean this compassionately.

And if there's anyone here that came on wheels tonight, anyone with a hint of chrome, a touch of Richard III about them, please, I'm *not* a healer. I have to say this, I cannot heal. Oh how I wish I could heal, but I can't. I'm sorry, but I can't. So don't bring your sore bits round to me later.

After her chat with the audience came the chat-show on stage as selected possums dressed up as freaks – a nun, an ancient punk, the Queen Mother – gulped Australian champagne and absorbed Edna's insults ('I bet you were once an attractive woman'), including a tense if hilarious moment as her flickering eye (which Nancy Banks-Smith likened to a Black and Decker drill) and her twitching mouth show that she has nothing to say to these nonentities. The gladdie finale brought the sensation of the night as Edna in a fork-lift ascended to the gods Was it a parody of the Assumption of the Virgin? The Resurrection? Michael Ratcliffe reported simply: 'Breathtaking'. For Sheridan Morley, this apotheosis, with Edna looking like a demented goddess from a harvest festival, reached 'a level of such gothic eccentricity as to render further attempts at analysis utterly futile'. She was now more than a megastar, she had become, if not a goddess, an icon (with, as she said 'street credibility'). Why should she not be the Church of England's first female saint? Has there ever been, she inquired without subtlety, a woman Pope?

20

A Bit of Stick

Early in 1959 in the obscure and now largely lost pages of a
Melbourne little magazine, the *Contemporary Art Society
Broadsheet*, an explosive, thirty-five-year-old surrealist painter, Ian Sime, published a polemic, 'Humpf-bumpf', which
set the tone for decades of Australian criticism of Barry
Humphries by those who believed that they were the targets
of his satire. Sime, as confident, eloquent, loquacious and
splenetic as many of Humphries' characters, saw himself as a
humanist anarchist who spoke for 'the thinking heart', for
the 'basic yearning for a universal human community of
love', as celebrated, he said, by Marcel Duchamp, Tristan
Tzara, Paul Klee, Jean Giono and Roberto Matta! He
despised the petty, the prejudiced and the pretentious, and
had just returned to Melbourne from northern Australia
where he had taught Aboriginal children to write in
medieval script so that they might cock a calligraphic snoot,
as he put it, at the poisonously racist lower-middle-class
incompetents who ran the local government and schools. 'I
have returned,' he wrote, 'from a bored exile' to find that his
home town, which had once espoused the cause of art and
compassion, had enthroned a 'vicious idiocy', that is, a cult
of Barry Humphries.

Humphries is no satirist of moral and social evils, Sime
His is a sick mind and 'the Humphrey [*sic*] tree has
only the stunted bitter berries of personal

vindictiveness', to the embarrassment and discomfort of his audiences. His 'resentful, juvenile gloating over the maimed, the feeble and the moronic [is] the result of a deep sense of inadequacy comforting itself by the sight of other, more obviously inadequate, human wrecks and accidents.' As for Humphries' hatred of women, his fear of homosexuals, and his 'savage lampooning of an obvious mother image' in Mrs Everage, Sime declared: 'Adolescence is a time of rather turgid emotional stresses and of some attempt to solve the mother-son relationships – of finally severing the cord. But to continue this essentially private and temporary condition into adulthood and public life is both boring and unneccessary. There are good simple cures available today for the emotional and physical acne of puberty – and the public exhibition of self-inflicted sores, is, I have always thought, a sign of backward countries and minds.' Sime concluded his article ominously: *To be continued.*

In the next issue of the *Broadsheet* a twenty-one-year-old Tony Morphett, later to become a prominent writer, briskly dismissed Sime's rodomontade. Sime's proclaimed love of humanity was, he wrote, far too broad, and Morphett reserved the right to hate the 'demagogues, bomb-droppers and book-burners'. As for Humphries, his 'big hate' was obviously for 'the lying and the crap and the carry-on' of modern life, and Morphett shared it. In any case, you do not presume to dictate themes to an artist, including a comic artist.

But if Morphett disposed of Sime's polemic, this sort of exchange has continued almost annually in Australia, in almost the same terms, for the past thirty years. Few actors in the history of the theatre have been so repeatedly attacked by commentators as Humphries, and the attacks have grown sharper as his popularity has increased. The argument received its most elaborate expression in the 1980s in a debate between Craig McGregor in the *National Times* and Hal Colebatch in *Quadrant*. Craig McGregor – a prize-winning New Journalist, novelist, rock-opera librettist, Bob Dylan scholar, and prolific author of a range of books from *This Surfing Life* to *Up Against the Wall, America* – has been a persistent critic of Humphries ever since Humphries' breakthrough in his show *Excuse I* in 1965 when Neil Singleton joined Edna and Sandy in the Humphriesian family. In that year McGregor found Humphries' satire to be 'rooted in a profound anti-humanism', the final proof of which was the book *Bizarre* which was an attempt to 'demean ordinary life'.

A few years later he went further: Humphries was 'very sick' with 'a special sort of arrogance'. His *Bizarre* was merely 'Port Said perviness between hard covers', and Humphries himself, however brilliant, was 'just another clown'. But his principal critique was in 1982 after a visit to a Humphries show at a poker-machine casino on the Gold Coast. There, he reported, was Humphries, still 'cracking his racist jokes, pillorying pinkos, Abos, unionists and of course women'. He continues to turn 'the full and bilious force of his contempt upon the losers and defenceless in society ... Abos, Jews, migrants, unionists, feminists, the great mass of common people'. Where is his satire on the Australian (then conservative) Government with its 'tax evasion scandals, questionable take-overs and business manoeuvres, government corruption ...?' Where are the satires on businessmen? McGregor repeated his earlier view about Humphries' 'profound anti-humanism', but this time he also found him 'profoundly reactionary', with a 'deep and abiding contempt for the human race' and a total hatred of Australia. With his 'constant pillorying of the Left', Humphries 'is habitually on the wrong side' and there is 'the stink' of fear and loathing in his work which evoked the grotesque and despairing cabaret of Berlin as the Nazis began their climb to power. Surprisingly he then concluded: 'as I've said before, just ʼher clown'.

ʼter-blast the poet and novelist Hal Colebatch

dealt with McGregor in a greater detail then Morphett could have called on in the 1950s when Humphries was a beginner. It is not the losers, he pointed out, but the winners who receive the full force of Humphries' rage — trendy frauds, wealthy opportunists, men who have 'lost their capacity to see women other than as sexual objects, parents unable to see children other than as ego-symbols and children unable to see parents other than as meal tickets'.

There is nothing scornful of Aborigines or immigrants in Humphries' shows, except in the mouths of characters intended to be 'contemptible, stupid or repulsively unsympathetic', and there is absolutely nothing at all that can be taken to be contemptuous of Jews. Humphries' target, Colebatch argued like Morphett years before, is 'the unformed and unfeeling heart', and his values are not far from those associated with E.M.Forster. Humphries does desire Australia to be a more genuinely civilized society and he 'sees the pretentious trendies who infest its media and educational establishments as betrayers of a great trust, namely, the fostering and transmitting of the best ideas in civilization'. Perhaps Humphries would do well to give more prominence to 'the good, the decent, and the noble', but Colebatch concluded, again like Morphett years before, 'I do not think this is a matter on which one can advise an artist without being foolishly presumptuous'.

There have been other and different complaints about Humphries' art over the years. Early in his career he was often dismissed as a coterie comedian, as too intellectual to be popular, as a flash in the pan. When those criticisms could not be sustained, he was dismissed as dated or anachronistic. Then he was denounced as an unpatriotic scandal: one critic, from the depths of his indignation, thundered that Humphries was no longer an Australian and had become a Londoner! But the perennial attack has been the Sime-McGregor one and the defence a Morphett-Colebatch one, with dozens of participants on both sides. The argument shows no sign of ending; each time one critic points out that Humphries' target is 'the lying and the crap and the carry-on', the unfeeling heart and the unformed mind, another steps forward to declare that Humphries is sick, vindictive, nihilistic and probably fascist. But it may still be possible to add something to this dialogue of the deaf.

Humphries himself will not directly contribute much to these polemics, from which he has sensibly kept his distance: 'So much of what a comedian does is instinct. Intellectualism explains nothing except to the humourless. It's like trying to explain music.' Occasionally, perhaps goaded by some humourless attack, he has remarked that his main target is himself, that his mockery is self-mockery, that humour can never spring out of hatred, and that nothing in the world is worse than an arrogant comedian. Once or twice he has replied to a critic. When reviewing *In the Making*, a book on Australian artists edited by Craig McGregor, he wrote:

> Unhappily I lack Mr McGregor's fabled reticence, but must in all justice acknowledge that this youthful and sincere champion of aquatic recreations (temporarily turned critic) has elsewhere and with obsessional vigour discussed my antics, though to be fair our deft journalist is but a ham-fisted lepidopterist and his wildly thrashing butterfly net has thus far failed to snare this glittering fritillary of the footlights.

He ended the review with a derisive solemnity: 'We share the editor's [i.e. McGregor's] sense of awe and wonderment, for the creative gift is a very mysterious, even suspect ⸱henomenon, *particularly to those untouched by it.*'

⸱ occasions when a critic offers some faint praise ⸱⸱mnation (as McGregor did in 1968 when he

took time to describe Neil Singleton as a perceptive creation
before dismissing Humphries as 'just another clown')
Humphries would remark: 'Yes, Martin Agrippa collects
Barry Humphries records'.

He prefers to be seen, not as a satirist ('Norm and I adore
satire, and yoga', Edna said crushingly at the height of the
satire boom in the 1960s), but as an entertainer who has
already amused more than two generations, refuting his own
cool dictum: 'A generation later, a comic is never funny'.
'Far from wishing to change society,' he once wrote,
obviously enjoying his lines, 'I can only hope that my
audience will pause, reflect for a moment, and pass on their
immutable way, not forgetting, perhaps, to drop a coin in
my hat.' But there is far more to it than this – although only
the pompous could undervalue the sheer hilarity, zaniness
and pathos of his shows or burden them with too much
tedious 'relevance' and heavy 'point of view'. Yet many
critics have sensed amid the helpless laughter a whiff of
sulphur, a hint of Savonarola, an echo of howling rage.
Humphries himself has conceded on one occasion, wearing a
different mask: 'I have said that I do not wish to edify, that
there is no moral purpose in my work. I lie when I say that.
There *is* a moral purpose. I do want to change things.' He wants
to give us – and himself – a bit of stick, like his Methodist
forefathers in Lancashire. 'That's what they enjoy. You can
hear them panting like old Swinburne in the flagellants' brothel:
Harder! Harder!' Yet however Swiftian he may be, he stops
short of seeing mankind as odious vermin. His world is a chill
and suffering one, but not without hope.

Observers have often commented on the mood of Humphries' audiences as they leave the theatre – stunned,
bemused, perplexed or disoriented. They certainly do not
write about these audiences in the way James Agate wrote
about those of Marie Lloyd, the music-hall comedienne who
fascinated T.S.Eliot. 'No one left the theatre,' Agate wrote

with relief, 'feeling spiritually better. From that blight at least, they were free.' Humphries' audiences, however, are in some sense clearly 'blighted'.

For example, the English reviewer John Elsom regarded *Housewife-Superstar*! in 1976 as not only brilliant entertainment but as 'good theatre', as life-changing: 'It makes us,' he said, *'think and feel differently afterwards.'* Partly this is because Humphries exposes the loudmouths and bullies, the humbugs and racketeers, the sots and pseuds who seem to have the run of the world. He liberates us from our confusion and we see things plainly for once. But there is also something closer to the bone. The Australian critic Katherine Brisbane examined her own response to *Isn't It Pathetic At His Age* in 1978 in this way: her feelings were, she said, ambivalent. She felt 'exploited' and 'slightly soiled' by the way the characters invited her to laugh callously and to obey absurd calls to wave gladdies. 'And yet ... within that mixture of laughter and revulsion I believe that Humphries has once more placed his finger upon what we still find most disturbing about our apparently liberated society. And it is that moment when the laughter stops that we come to recognize this.'

Humphries invites us to look – with him – into a mirror and we see Caliban. We acknowledge and we give up, however briefly, some of the lies we live by. This may either relieve or unsettle us, or both. Humphries described the audience's reaction in 1962 to Mrs Everage's bigoted barb ('They get all the best places, don't they?') about Roman Catholic building sites: 'You would notice immediately the prejudice flowing out, the feeling of relief like a boil being lanced. I don't think I'll ever get a gag as good as that again.' When the trade union racketeer Lance Boyle first appeared 1978 in all his left-wing fascism, the audience responded shocked sucking-in of air; it was, Humphries said, a w sound, 'like a copy of the *Canberra Times* going ney'. But it is not a negative or nihilist experience. When Dame Edna calls the shows 'a massage parlour of the human spirit', she is, beneath the several layers of irony, right.

Humphries' passion as an artist (or his Dada daemon's) has been from the beginning in the 1950s to loosen the grip on us all (including himself) of diminishing assumptions, to get us to see ourselves and the world in a different way, one closer to the truth. This passion animated his youthful street theatre, the Dada hoaxes, however poorly executed, and it animates the one-man shows in packed theatres today. Humphries does not preach a moral doctrine (Sandy's wheezing of the Lord's Prayer is both less and more) but there is always the will to grasp things 'as they really are', a glimmer of truth that is the beginning of the restoration of civility.

Laughter is inevitable. As Humphries put it: 'If you're on stage and telling the truth – however it may be disguised poetically or comically, however it may verge on caricature or fantasy – if it is *fundamentally truthful* laughter will be there – it is the noise of recognition.' But not only laughter. There may be something like sobbing: Humphries is always close to sorrow and we all stand with Sandy in the cold and blowy outer. It is Barry Humphries' genius that he can, through laughter and tears, restore to us, if only for a moment, a suggestion of sanity, a hint of hope, a rumour of revival.

Selected Works of Barry Humphries

SHOWS

Call Me Madman! With Melbourne Dada Group, Union Theatre, Melbourne, 1952
Return Fare Union Theatre, Melbourne, 1955
Mr and Mrs Phillip Street Theatre, Sydney, 1956
Around the Loop Phillip Street Theatre, Sydney, 1956–7
Waiting for Godot With Peter O'Shaughnessy, Arrow Theatre, Melbourne, 1957
   Independent Theatre, Sydney, 1958
The Bunyip and the Satellite With Peter O'Shaughnessy, National Theatre, Melbourne, 1957
   Independent Theatre, Sydney, 1958
Rock 'n' Reel Revue With Peter O'Shaughnessy, New Theatre, Melbourne, 1958
The Demon Barber Lyric, Hammersmith, London, 1959
Oliver! New Theatre, London, 1960
   Imperial Theater, New York, 1963
   Piccadilly Theatre, London, 1967
A Nice Night's Entertainment Australian tour, 1962
The Bed-Sitting Room The Duke of York's Theatre, London, 1963
Barry Humphries The Establishment Club, London, 1963
Merry Rooster's Panto Wyndham's Theatre, London, 1963
A Kayf Up West Theatre Royal, Stratford East, 1964

Maggie May Adelphi Theatre, London, 1964

Excuse I Australian tour, 1965

Treasure Island Mermaid Theatre, London 1967

Just a Show Australian tour, 1968
Fortune Theatre, London, 1969

A Load of Olde Stuffe Australian tour, 1971

At Least You Can Say You've Seen It Australian tour, 1974

Housewife-Superstar! Apollo and Globe Theatres, London, 1976; Theatre Four, New York, 1977

Isn't It Pathetic At His Age Australian tour, 1978

A Night with Dame Edna. Piccadilly Theatre, London, 1978–9. (Winner of the London Society of West End Managements' Award for Comedy Performance of the Year, 1979)

An Evening's Intercourse with Barry Humphries Regent Theatre, Sydney, and then Her Majesty's Theatre, Melbourne, 1981; Theatre Royal, Drury Lane, London, 1982

Last Night of the Poms With Carl Davis, Albert Hall, London, 1982; then as *Song of Australia* Regent Theatre, Sydney, and Melbourne Concert Hall, 1983

Tears Before Bedtime Australian tour, 1985; then as

Back With a Vengeance Strand Theatre, London, 1987–8

The Life and Death of Sandy Stone Australian tour, 1990

BOOKS

Bizarre Elek Books, London, 1965

The Barry Humphries Book of Innocent Austral Verse Sun Books, Melbourne, 1968

The Wonderful World of Barry McKenzie With Nicholas Garland, *Private Eye*/André Deutsch, London, 1969

Bazza Pulls It Off With Nicholas Garland, Sun Books, Melbourne, 1972

The Adventures of Barry McKenzie With Bruce Beresford, Sun Books, Melbourne, 1973

Bazza Holds His Own With Nicholas Garland, Sun Books, Melbourne, 1974

Dame Edna's Coffee Table Book Harrap, London, 1976

Bazza Comes Into His Own With Nicholas Garland, Sun Books, Melbourne, 1978

Les Patterson's Australia Sun Books, Melbourne, 1979

Barry Humphries' Treasury of Australian Kitsch Macmillan, Melbourne, 1980

A Nice Night's Entertainment. Sketches and Monologues 1956–1981 Currency Press, Sydney, 1981, Granada, London, 1981

Dame Edna's Bedside Companion Weidenfeld & Nicolson, London, 1982

The Humour of Barry Humphries. Selections by John Allen, Currency Press, 1984

The Traveller's Tool, Sir Les Patterson Macmillan, Melbourne, 1985

The Complete Barry McKenzie With Nicholas Garland, Methuen, London; Allen & Unwin, Sydney, 1988

Shades of Sandy Stone The Tragara Press, Edinburgh, 1989

My Gorgeous Life, Dame Edna Everage Macmillan, Melbourne 1989

The Life and Death of Sandy Stone. Edited by Collin O'Brien, Macmillan, Melbourne, 1990

DISCS

Wild Life in Suburbia 1. Edna Everage: *The Migrant Hostess* 2. Sandy Stone: *Days of the Week,* 1958

Wild Life in Suburbia, volume two. 1. Edna Everage: *Highett Fidelity* 2. Sandy Stone: *Dear Beryl,* 1959

Sandy Agonistes 1. Buster Thompson. 2. Debbie Thwaite. 3. Colin Cartwright. 4. Sandy Stone: *Sandy Agonistes,* 1960

A Nice Night's Entertainment 1. Edna Everage: *Australian* ...... (live recording) 2. Edna Everage: *Meets Friends Old*

and New. 3. Sandy Stone: *Can You Keep a Secret?* 1960
Chunder Down Under 1. *Snow Complications*. 2. *The Old Pacific Sea*, 1965
Barry Humphries 1. Sandy Stone: *Days of the Week* 2. Edna Everage: *War Savings Street Song* (rec. 1962) 3. Debbie Thwaite. 4. *Chunder Down Under*, 1970
Barry Humphries' Savoury Dip 1. Edna Everage: *Edna's Hymn* 2. *Wendy the One-Eyed Wombat* 3. Edna Everage: *The Highett Waltz*. 4. *Great Big Fish*. 5. Barry Humphries at Las Vegas: *What is a Ratbag?* 6. Sandy Stone: *Sandy Claus*, 1971
The Barry Humphries Record of Innocent Austral Verse, 1972
A Track Winding Back 1. *Along the Road to Gundagai* (duet, Barry Humphries with Dick Bentley) 2. *Is 'E an Aussie, Is 'E, Lizzie* (duet, Barry Humphries with Dick Bentley) 3. Edna Everage: *True British Spunk*, 1972
Barry Humphries at Carnegie Hall 1. Edna Everage: *First Day Covers* (music by Nigel Butterley; John Hopkins conducting the Sydney Symphony Orchestra) 2. Sandy Stone: *Sandy's Stone* 3. Sandy Stone: *Sandy Sings Sacred Songs*, 1972
Housewife-Superstar! Recorded live at the Globe Theatre, London, 8 July 1976. 1. Les Patterson. 2. Edna Everage, 1976
The Sound of Edna, 1978
Twelve Inches of Les, 1985

TELEVISION SHOWS

Wild Life and Christmas Belles, Melbourne, 1958
Trip-Tease and High C's, Melbourne, 1959
Comfort Station, Melbourne, 1966
The Barry Humphries Scandals, London, 1970
The Barry Humphries Show, London, 1976
A Summer Sideshow, London, 1977
An Audience with Dame Edna, London, 1980
Another Audience with Dame Edna, London, 1984

An Aussie Audience with Dame Edna, Melbourne, 1986
The Dame Edna Experience, London, 1987
Dame Edna's Christmas Experience, London, 1987
One More Audience with Dame Edna, London, 1988

FILMS

Bedazzled, 1967
The Adventures of Barry McKenzie, 1972
Barry McKenzie Holds His Own, 1974
The Great McCarthy, 1974
The Getting of Wisdom, 1977
Dr Fischer of Geneva, 1984
Les Patterson Saves the World, 1987

ART EXHIBITIONS

The First Pan-Australasian Dada Exhibition, Melbourne, 1952.
The Second Pan-Australasian Dada Exhibition, Melbourne, 1953.
Barry Humphries. Victorian Artists Society Gallery, Melbourne, 1958.
Ten Little Australians, Myer Mural Hall, Melbourne, 1968.
Barry Humphries Retrospective, Bonython Galleries, Sydney, 1968.
A Brief Glimpse. Barry Humphries the Painter, Golden Crust Gallery, Melbourne, 1989.

Index

187

ROBERT MORLEY
AROUND THE WORLD IN 81 YEARS

It all started at Folkestone.

'On rough days Nurse would take us down to the harbour ... where we found sea-sick passengers in a woebegone huddle boarding waiting trains. "That's what comes of going abroad, Master Robert," she would tell me.'

But to Act is perforce to Travel.

The young Robert Morley, learning his craft in provincial touring companies, discovers that in England all journeys involve a Sunday afternoon change at Crewe.

Later come location shoots in exotic foreign parts with exotic foreign weather. Nature, he realises abhors the film maker and teases the tourist. Ayers Rock resolutely refuses to turn pink at dawn. The Niagara Falls are closed for repairs ...

Around the World in 81 Years is a delightful voyage through times and places, packed with anecdotes and asides, by a man who loves life but basically finds it all part of the theatre of the absurd.

'A delight to leaf through ... the perfect travelling companion'   *Film Review*

HODDER AND STOUGHTON PAPERBACKS